Academic VOCABULARY Toolkit

Mastering High-Use Words for Academic Achievement

Dr. Kate Kinsella

with Theresa Hancock

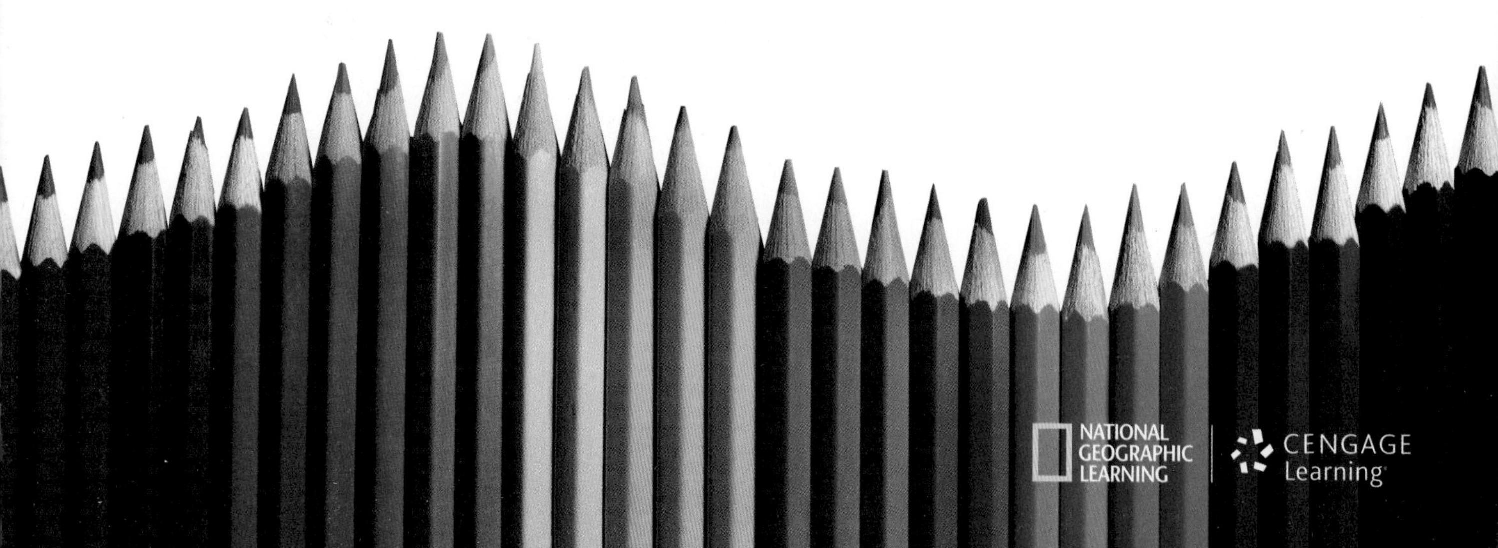

NATIONAL GEOGRAPHIC LEARNING | CENGAGE Learning

Acknowledgments
Grateful acknowledgment is given to the authors, artists, photographers, museums, publishers, and agents for permission to reprint copyrighted material. Every effort has been made to secure the appropriate permission. If any omissions have been made or if corrections are required, please contact the publisher.

Photographic Credits:
Front Cover ©Victoria Ivanova/500px Prime.
iv (t) ©spotmatik/Shutterstock.com, (cr) ©Nikolai Pozdeev/Shutterstock.com, (cl) ©Alinute Silzeviciute/Shutterstock.com, (b) ©Olesya Feketa/Shutterstock.com.

Text Credits:
22 "Green Sea Turtle" from *National Geographic Society* online.

Acknowledgments and credits continue on page 180.

For product information and technology assistance, contact us at **Customer & Sales Support, 888-915-3276**

For permission to use material from this text or product, submit all requests online at **www.cengage.com/permissions**
Further permissions questions can be emailed to **permissionrequest@cengage.com**

National Geographic Learning | Cengage Learning
1 Lower Ragsdale Drive
Building 1, Suite 200
Monterey, CA 93940

Cengage Learning is a leading provider of customized learning solutions with office locations around the globe, including Singapore, the United Kingdom, Australia, Mexico, Brazil, and Japan. Locate your local office at **www.cengage.com/global**.

Cengage Learning products are represented in Canada by Nelson Education, Ltd.

Visit National Geographic Learning online at **NGL.Cengage.com**
Visit our corporate website at **www.cengage.com**

Printed in the USA.
RR Donnelley, Menasha, WI, USA

ISBN: 9781305079106

Printed in the United States of America
17 18 19 20 21 22 23
13 12 11 10 9 8 7 6

Contents at a Glance

Unit 1
Describe

Unit 2
Analyze Informational Text

RVICES

Unit 3
Cause and Effect

SMART START

Unit 4
Sequence

SMART START

Unit 5
Create

Unit 6
Compare and Contrast

Unit 7
Inference

Unit 8
Argument

Toolkit Unit 1 | Describe

Describe

To **describe** a person, explain how he or she looks, acts, and what the person says. If possible, include what others think or say about the person.

To **describe** a location or a thing, use your senses to explain how it looks, feels, smells, sounds, and tastes.

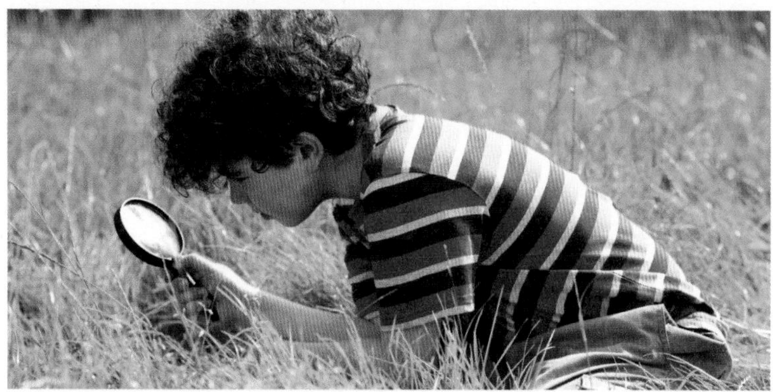

 **Find It** **Read the sentences below and underline the words that describe a person, thing, or location.**

1. My cousin Tina is my best friend. She is tall and has very curly brown hair. Each day she wears a different color headband to keep her hair off her face. Tina loves to talk about soccer and horses. Everyone says that Tina is helpful and friendly.

2. I love my new bike. It is red and has thick, bumpy wheels. It has six speeds. You change the gears by twisting the grip on the right-hand handlebar. When I ride my bike, I feel confident and free. I love to ride fast through puddles after it rains.

 **Try It** **Think about one person you know. Write one important detail in each section of the chart that you would use to describe the person.**

RATE WORD KNOWLEDGE

Circle the number that shows your knowledge of the words you'll use to describe people, places, and things.

RATE IT

BEFORE	3rd Grade	AFTER	4th Grade	5th Grade
1 2 3 4	**type**	1 2 3 4	character	description
1 2 3 4	**behavior**	1 2 3 4	trait	aspect
1 2 3 4	**physical**	1 2 3 4	appearance	quality
1 2 3 4	**personality**	1 2 3 4	include	characteristic
1 2 3 4	**contain**	1 2 3 4	experience	illustrate
1 2 3 4	**event**	1 2 3 4	location	respond

DISCUSSION GUIDE

- Form groups of four.
- Assign letters to each person.
- Each group member takes a turn leading a discussion.
- Prepare to report about one word.

Ⓐ Ⓑ
Ⓓ Ⓒ

DISCUSS WORDS

Discuss how well you know the third grade words. Then, report to the class how you rated each word.

GROUP LEADER **Ask**

So, ________ (NAME) what do you know about the word ________ ?

GROUP MEMBERS **Discuss**

1 = I **have never seen or heard** the word ________ . I need to learn what it means.

2 = I **have seen or heard** the word ________ , but I need to learn the meaning.

3 = I'm **familiar** with the word ________ . I think it means ________ .

4 = I **know** the word ________ . It means ________ .

REPORTER **Report Word Knowledge**

Our group gave the word ________ a rating of ________ .

SET A GOAL AND REFLECT

First, set a vocabulary goal for this unit by selecting at least two words that you plan to thoroughly learn. At the end of the unit, return to this page and write a reflection about one word you have mastered.

GOAL

During this unit I plan to thoroughly learn the words ________ and ________ . Increasing my word knowledge will help me speak and write effectively when I describe a person, location, or ________ .

REFLECTION

As a result of this unit, I feel most confident about the word ________ . This is my model sentence: ________ ________ .

type

noun

Say it: type

Write it: ______________ ***Write it again:*** ______________

____

TOOLKIT

Meaning

a group of things or people that are like each other in some way

Synonym

- kind

Examples

- In the United States, dogs and cats are the most popular **types** of ___________ .

- My favorite **type** of snack is an ___________ .

Forms

- **Singular:** type
- **Past:** types

Family

- **Adjective:** typical

Word Partners

- many types of
- type of ___________

Examples

- Our class talked about **many types of** stories before we decided on the book we would read next.
- The Tyrannosaurus rex is a **type of dinosaur** scientists know a lot about.

Try It

My favorite **type** of activity at recess is playing ______________________ because I am really good at it.

VERBAL PRACTICE

Talk about it **Discuss ideas with your partner, listen to classmates, and then write your favorite idea.**

Discuss
Listen
Write

1. The **types** of TV shows I like to watch most are the ones about ______________________________ .

2. Many third-grade students like to draw pictures of different **types** of ______________________________ in stories.

type

noun

WRITING PRACTICE

Collaborate

Discuss
Listen
Agree
Write

Discuss ideas with your partner and agree on the best words to complete the frame.

Our teacher described three ________________ of prizes students might receive during the ________________________ at the end of the year.

Our Turn

Discuss
Listen
Write

Read the prompt. Work with the teacher to complete the frames. Write a thoughtful response that includes a reason.

PROMPT: What is one type of dessert that students would enjoy during a class party?

One ________________________ of dessert students would enjoy during a class party is ______________________. Many third graders love eating __________________________________, so it would be an ideal treat.

Be an Academic Author

Write
Discuss
Listen

Read the prompt and complete the frames. Strengthen your response with a reason.

PROMPT: What are your favorite types of books to read?

My favorite __________________________ of books to read are about ________________________. I enjoy reading these books because they make me feel ____.

Construct a Response

Read
Discuss
Listen

Read the prompt and write a thoughtful response. Strengthen your response with a reason.

PROMPT: Some families like to visit relatives during their vacations. Other families like to visit new places. What type of vacation do you like best?

____

____

____.

grammar tip

Count nouns name things that can be counted. Count nouns have two forms, singular and plural. To make most count nouns plural, add **-s**.

EXAMPLE: Most **students** enjoy talking and playing with their **friends** during recess.

behavior

noun

Say it: be • **hav** • ior

Write it: ______________ ***Write it again:*** ______________

____

TOOLKIT

Meaning

the way a person talks and acts, or things an animal does

Synonym

- actions

Examples

- Because of his courageous **behavior**, my cousin got an ______________ from the mayor.

- A dog wagging his tail is a **behavior** that means he is ______________ .

Forms

- **Singular:** behavior
- **Plural:** behaviors

Family

- **Verb:** behave

Word Partners

- good/bad behavior
- typical behavior

Examples

- Saying "Please" and "Thank you" are two examples of **good behavi**
- Screaming when they are angry is **typical behavior** for three-year-olds.

Try It

The principal noticed our good **behavior** during the assembly, so she gave us tickets for two free ______________ .

VERBAL PRACTICE

Talk about it **Discuss ideas with your partner, listen to classmates, and then write your favorite idea.**

Discuss
Listen
Write

1. Most children show polite **behavior** when they go to (a/an) ______________ ______________ .

2. I know that my friend is in a bad mood when her **behavior** changes and she starts to ______________ .

behavior

noun

WRITING PRACTICE

Collaborate

Discuss
Listen
Agree
Write

Discuss ideas with your partner and agree on the best words to complete the frame.

At the end of the ______________________, the detective explained that the thief's suspicious ______________________ showed that he was guilty.

Our Turn

Discuss
Listen
Write

Read the prompt. Work with the teacher to complete the frames. Write a thoughtful response that includes an example.

PROMPT: What is one type of good behavior that you would want in a new friend?

One type of good ______________________ that I would want in a new friend is being ______________________. For example, having a new friend who tries to ______________________ would be great.

Be an Academic Author

Write
Discuss
Listen

Read the prompt and complete the frames. Strengthen your response with an example.

PROMPT: Imagine that you are going to write a story about a popular superhero. What is one typical behavior that shows the superhero's special talent?

In my story about the popular superhero, ______________________, I would describe how (he/she) ______________ is able to ______________________. This typical ______________________ shows the superhero's special talent.

Construct a Response

Read
Discuss
Listen

Read the prompt and write a thoughtful response. Strengthen your response with an example.

PROMPT: Imagine you are going to write a story about an unhappy character. How would you describe the character's bad behavior to show that he or she is unhappy?

____

____

______________________.

grammar tip

An **adjective** describes, or tells about, a noun. Usually an adjective goes before the noun.

EXAMPLE: The **colorful** clown danced and told **silly** jokes.

physical

adjective

Say it: phys • i • cal

 ***Write it:*** ____________ ***Write it again:*** ____________

 ____________

TOOLKIT

Meaning

related to what a person, animal, or object is made of or looks like

Examples

- One **physical** activity some families enjoy together is riding ____________.

- The most obvious **physical** feature of a giraffe is its long ____________.

Family

- **Adverb:** physically

Word Partners

- physical activity
- physical feature

Examples

- Experts say that you should get at least 60 minutes of **physical activity** each day to have good health.
- My baby brother can name three of his **physical features**: his nose, his eyes, and his ears.

 **Try It**

During recess, one **physical** activity I enjoy is ____________

VERBAL PRACTICE

Talk about it Discuss Listen Write

Discuss ideas with your partner, listen to classmates, and then write your favorite idea.

1. Two **physical** features of a car are the windshield and the ____________.

2. After falling from the ____________ at the park, the boy had several **physical** marks, such as scrapes and bruises on his arms.

WRITING PRACTICE

Collaborate
Discuss
Listen
Agree
Write

Discuss ideas with your partner and agree on the best words to complete the frame.

Guess which object has these ______________ features: four legs and a flat top. What is it? It's a ______________.

Our Turn
Discuss
Listen
Write

Read the prompt. Work with the teacher to complete the frames. Write a thoughtful response that includes a reason.

PROMPT: Imagine a story about a superhero named Superwolf. What physical feature would you describe? Why would that feature be important in the story?

The ______________ features I would describe would be Superwolf's special ears and strong ______________. These would help Superwolf hear and ______________ enemies.

Be an Academic Author
Write
Discuss
Listen

Read the prompt and complete the frames. Strengthen your response with a reason.

PROMPT: What is your favorite physical activity during the weekend? Why do you enjoy the activity?

On weekends, my favorite ______________ activity is playing ______________. I enjoy this activity because I get to ______________ a lot.

Construct a Response
Read
Discuss
Listen

Read the prompt and write a thoughtful response. Strengthen your response with a reason.

PROMPT: Do you have a favorite toy? Describe its most important physical feature.

____

____

______________.

grammar tip

A **common noun** names a person, place, animal, thing, or idea. Singular nouns name one person, place, animal, thing, or idea. The words *a*, *an*, and *the* appear before a singular noun.

EXAMPLE: The **cat** chased a **mouse** across the **kitchen** and into a **hole** in the **wall**.

personality

noun

Say it: per • son • **al** • ity

 ***Write it:*** ______________ ***Write it again:*** ______________

 ______________

TOOLKIT

Meaning

the type of person you are and the way you act around others

Synonym

- character

Examples

- Our school nurse has a ______________ **personality**.

- Because of her funny **personality**, my cousin has many ______________ .

Forms

- **Singular:** personality
- **Plural:** personalities

Word Partners	Examples
• has (a/an) outgoing/ weak personality	• Someone who **has an outgoing personality** likes to meet many new people.
• (his/her) pleasant/ unpleasant personality	• Many kids dislike the bully in the cartoon because of **his unpleasant personality**.

 **Try It**

A person who pushes and cuts in line generally has a ______________ **personality**.

VERBAL PRACTICE

Talk about it

Discuss
Listen
Write

Discuss ideas with your partner, listen to classmates, and then write your favorite idea.

1. Most elementary school students enjoy a teacher with (a/an) ______________

______________ **personality**.

2. The handsome or beautiful hero of an exciting movie usually has (a/an) ______________

______________ **personality**.

personality

noun

WRITING PRACTICE

Collaborate

Discuss
Listen
Agree
Write

Discuss ideas with your partner and agree on the best words to complete the frame.

To write funny ______________________, you need to have a bubbly or clever ______________________ and enjoy making people laugh.

Our Turn

Discuss
Listen
Write

Read the prompt. Work with the teacher to complete the frames. Write a thoughtful response that includes a reason.

PROMPT: Why should a dentist have a gentle personality?

A dentist should have a gentle ______________________ because most patients are ______________________ at the dentist's office. If the dentist is gentle, it helps the patients to ______________________.

Be an Academic Author

Write
Discuss
Listen

Read the prompt and complete the frames. Strengthen your response with a reason.

PROMPT: How would you describe your friend's personality? Why is this important to you?

I would describe my friend's ______________________ as ______________________. This is important to me because it makes me feel ______________________.

Construct a Response

Read
Discuss
Listen

Read the prompt and write a thoughtful response. Strengthen your response with a reason.

PROMPT: Who is your favorite movie character? Describe the character's personality.

____

____

______________________.

grammar tip

The **preposition *to*** needs to be followed by a base verb.

EXAMPLE: A good friend tells you **to try** hard and **to do** your best at all times.

contain

verb

Say it: con • **tain**

 ***Write it:*** ______________ ***Write it again:*** ______________

 ______________

TOOLKIT

Meaning

to have something inside

Synonym

- include

Examples

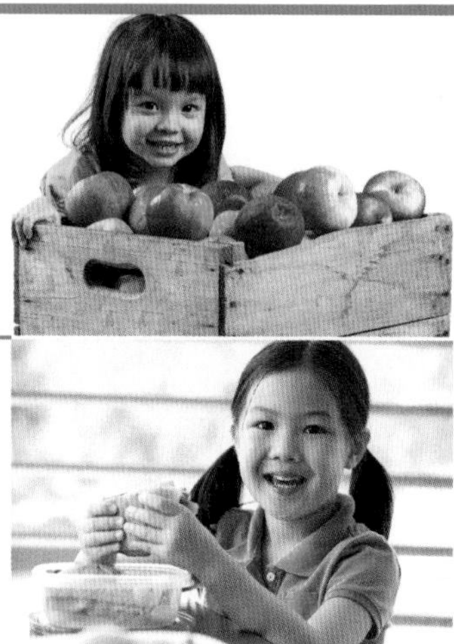

- My little cousin is hiding behind the box that **contains** a lot of ______________ .
- My lunch box **contains** grapes and a ______________ .

Forms

- **Present:**
  I/You/We/They contain
  He/She/It contains
- **Past:** contained

Family

- **Noun:** container

Word Partners

- contain a lot of
- do/does not contain any

Examples

- The book we're reading **contains a lot of** interesting characters.
- Since I have an allergy, our house does not contain any peanuts.

 **Try It**

Our school library **contains** a lot of books and ______________ .

VERBAL PRACTICE

Talk about it **Discuss ideas with your partner, listen to classmates, and then write your favorite idea.**

Discuss
Listen
Write

1. I do not enjoy eating ______________ because they **contain** a lot of seeds.

2. Our teacher's desk drawer does not **contain** any ______________ .

WRITING PRACTICE

Collaborate

Discuss
Listen
Agree
Write

Discuss ideas with your partner and agree on the best words to complete the frame.

Our dream house should ______________________ a room where we can

____.

Our Turn

Discuss
Listen
Write

Read the prompt. Work with the teacher to complete the frames. Write a thoughtful response that includes a reason.

PROMPT: What should a student's desk contain?

A student's desk should ______________________ several pencils and

______________________. Every student needs these items

to work on daily ______________________________.

Be an Academic Author

Write
Discuss
Listen

Read the prompt and complete the frames. Strengthen your response with a reason.

PROMPT: Most people like to imagine the perfect dessert. What two ingredients would your perfect dessert contain?

My perfect dessert would ______________________ these two ingredients:

______________________ and ______________________.

I would love this dessert because it would taste ______________________.

Construct a Response

Read
Discuss
Listen

Read the prompt and write a thoughtful response. Strengthen your response with a reason.

PROMPT: A time capsule contains things that are important at a certain time. What would your 3rd-grade time capsule contain?

____

____

____.

grammar tip

Use the **modal verb**, or helping verb, ***should*** to suggest or recommend something. When you use ***should***, add a verb in the base form.

EXAMPLE: Some teachers think that all students **should do** homework every night.

event

noun

Say it: e • vent

 ***Write it:*** ______________ ***Write it again:*** ______________

 ______________

TOOLKIT

Meaning

something important, interesting, or unusual that happens

Examples

- Going to a new ______________ was a big **event** in the girl's life.

- The birth of a new ______________ was a historic **event** in the family.

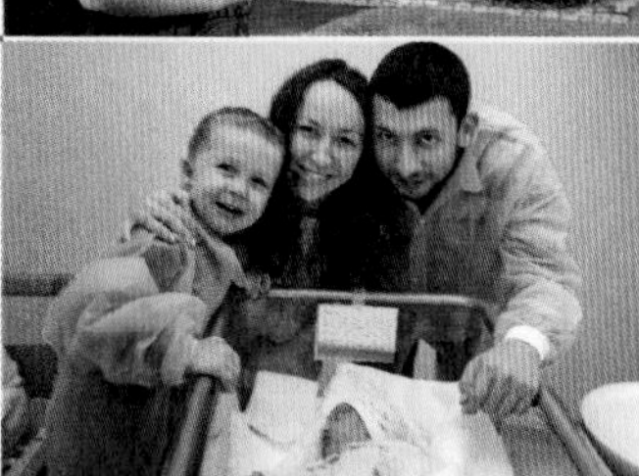

Forms

- **Singular:** event
- **Plural:** events

Word Partners	Examples
• a big event	• For any student, a birthday is **a big event** each year.
• a historic event	• The day humans walked on the moon for the first time was **a historic event** for the whole world.

 **Try It**

One **event** that happened last summer was going to the ______________ .

VERBAL PRACTICE

Talk about it

Discuss
Listen
Write

Discuss ideas with your partner, listen to classmates, and then write your favorite idea.

1. The day the famous ______________ came to our school was an **event** we will remember for a long time.

2. Our field trip to the ______________ might be the most exciting **event** this year.

event

noun

WRITING PRACTICE

Collaborate

Discuss
Listen
Agree
Write

Discuss ideas with your partner and agree on the best words to complete the frame.

For our science report, we chose one ______________________

in the life cycle of a frog and drew (a/an) ______________________

______________________ picture of it as a froglet.

Our Turn

Discuss
Listen
Write

Read the prompt. Work with the teacher to complete the frames. Write a thoughtful response that includes a reason.

PROMPT: What were two big events in the story of *Goldilocks and the Three Bears*?

One big ______________________ in *Goldilocks and the Three Bears* was when

Goldilocks first ______________________ the Bear's house.

Another big event happened when the Bears ______________________

Goldilocks sleeping in the bed that was just right.

Be an Academic Author

Write
Discuss
Listen

Read the prompt and complete the frames. Strengthen your response with a reason.

PROMPT: What is one big event that you enjoy at school? Why do you enjoy it?

One big ______________________ that I enjoy at school is the

______________________ . I enjoy this event because it shows how

creative and ______________________ the students are at our school.

Construct a Response

Read
Discuss
Listen

Read the prompt and write a thoughtful response. Strengthen your response with a reason.

PROMPT: What was one big event in your life? Why do you remember that event?

____

____

____ .

grammar tip

An **adjective** describes, or tells about, a noun. Usually an adjective goes before the noun.

EXAMPLE: The **beautiful** eagle spread its **large** wings as it flew away.

type

SMART START

REVIEW: **type** *noun*

DAY 1

I like to play many different ________________ of games, but my favorite game is ________________ because I am good at it.

type *noun*

DAY 2

One ________________ of snack that I like to eat after school is a delicious ________________.

DAY 3

At a zoo, you can see several ________________ of animals. For example, you can see huge apes, long crocodiles, and enormous ________________.

DAY 4

Our teacher asks us to do many different ________________ of writing. Sometimes we write stories. At other times we write ________________ reports.

DAY 5

My fantasy neighborhood has two ________________ of parks. One park has a swimming pool, and the other park has a big field where I can play ________________ with my friends.

TOTAL

REVIEW: type *noun*

DAY 1

My favorite ______________ of pizza is one with ______________.

behavior *noun*

DAY 2

One funny type of animal ______________ is the way a bird copies how people ______________.

DAY 3

Her grandfather's kind, helpful ______________ is one reason so many people ______________ him.

DAY 4

Telling a joke and making silly faces are typical ______________ I see when my best friend wants to make me ______________.

DAY 5

One way I can help my ______________ is by teaching younger children one kind of ______________ they should show in a classroom or at home.

TOTAL

physical

REVIEW: behavior *noun*

DAY 1

Most teachers require students to have good ______________________

during field trips, especially when visiting (a/an) ______________________

____.

physical *adjective*

DAY 2

My family's favorite ______________________ activity is

______________________________________ together.

DAY 3

The ____________________ feature of a tree that I notice first is its

____.

DAY 4

Our principal told us that 60 minutes of ______________________

activity each day is good for our ______________________.

DAY 5

Because of its special ____________________ features, a shark can

______________________________________ very well.

TOTAL

SMARTSTART

REVIEW: physical *adjective*

DAY 1

During P.E., my favorite ______ activity is playing ______ with my friends.

personality *noun*

DAY 2

To take care of ______ animals, a person must have a gentle and helpful ______.

DAY 3

Because my aunt has a creative and lively ______, everyone in our family wants to visit her every ______.

DAY 4

Our principal asked for a student volunteer who had a helpful ______ to show a new ______ around our school.

DAY 5

I think games like ______ are great for my friend because he has an outgoing and active ______.

TOTAL

contain

SMART START

REVIEW: personality *noun*

DAY 1

My best friend has a fun ______________________, and (he/she) ______________________ laughs when I tell ______________________ stories.

contain *verb*

DAY 2

Our classroom ______________________ desks, chairs, and lots of ______________________.

DAY 3

When packing for the picnic we decided to take an ice chest that ______________________ a lot of ice and ______________________.

DAY 4

Books for third graders should ______________________ stories about people, places, and ______________________ that no one expects.

DAY 5

My pockets often ______________________ many things, such as ______________________.

TOTAL

REVIEW: contain *verb*

DAY 1

My backpack always ______________________ many school supplies, including pencils and ______________________.

event *noun*

DAY 2

One big ______________________ I will never forget is the day my little cousin ______________________.

DAY 3

Awards Day is a big ______________________ in our school because so many parents and relatives come to see students receive well-deserved ______________________.

DAY 4

On the 4th of July, our community celebrates this historic ______________________ with a huge ______________________ in the park.

DAY 5

The day the new ______________________ opened was an exciting ______________________ in our town.

TOTAL

Toolkit Unit 2 | Analyze Informational Text

Analyze Informational Text

Analyze means to carefully study.

Informational text can be found in many places, such as articles in a newspaper, magazine, textbook, or even on the Internet. **Informational text** provides important information about something and includes facts.

To **analyze informational text**, be sure to:

- read the title and headings
- read each section, paragraph, or list many times
- carefully study any pictures and charts
- discuss key ideas and important details
- think about what you've learned

 **Find It** Read the sample texts below. Put a star next to the **informational text.**

from Turtle Beach Mystery

By Helen Moore

After dinner, the children sat out on the steps of the porch. Suddenly Josh exclaimed, "Alexis, look, a baby turtle! And there's another one by your leg. Watch out!"

"Whoa! What are they doing up here?" cried Alexis. "They're supposed to go out to sea."

"What's wrong with them?" Josh asked.

The Green Turtle

THE GREEN TURTLE is a large, weighty sea turtle with a wide, smooth carapace, or shell.

It is named not for the color of its shell, which is normally brown or olive depending on its habitat, but for the greenish color of its skin.

Weighing up to 700 pounds (317.5 kilograms), green turtles are among the largest sea turtles in the world. Males are slightly larger than females and have a longer tail. Both have flippers that resemble paddles, which make them powerful and graceful swimmers.

 **Try It** **Analyze** the informational text by reading it several times. Then underline important details, and discuss what you learned using the sentence frames.

One fact I learned from the informational text is that ______________________.

Another interesting detail I learned is that ______________________.

RATE WORD KNOWLEDGE

Circle the number that shows your knowledge of the words you'll use to analyze text.

RATE IT

BEFORE	3rd Grade	AFTER	4th Grade	5th Grade
1 2 3 4	**important**	1 2 3 4	focus	significant
1 2 3 4	**topic**	1 2 3 4	essential	section
1 2 3 4	**detail**	1 2 3 4	emphasize	discuss
1 2 3 4	**information**	1 2 3 4	precise	context
1 2 3 4	**fact**	1 2 3 4	message	excerpt
1 2 3 4	**example**	1 2 3 4	major	concept

DISCUSSION GUIDE

- Form groups of four.
- Assign letters to each person. Ⓐ Ⓑ Ⓓ Ⓒ
- Each group member takes a turn leading a discussion.
- Prepare to report about one word.

DISCUSS WORDS

Discuss how well you know the third grade words. Then, report to the class how you rated each word.

GROUP LEADER **Ask**

So, ________ (NAME) what do you know about the word ________?

GROUP MEMBERS **Discuss**

1 = I **have never seen or heard** the word ________. I need to learn what it means.

2 = I **have seen or heard** the word ________, but I need to learn the meaning.

3 = I'm **familiar** with the word ________. I think it means ________.

4 = I **know** the word ________. It means ________.

REPORTER **Report Word Knowledge**

Our group gave the word ________ a rating of ________.

SET A GOAL AND REFLECT

First, set a vocabulary goal for this unit by selecting at least two words that you plan to thoroughly learn. At the end of the unit, return to this page and write a reflection about one word you have mastered.

GOAL

During this unit I plan to completely learn the words ________ and ________. Increasing my word knowledge will help me speak and write effectively when I analyze informational ________.

REFLECTION

As a result of this unit, I feel most confident about the word ________. This is my model sentence: ________ ________.

important

adjective

Say it: im • **por** • tant

 ***Write it:*** ______________ ***Write it again:*** ______________

____

Meaning

something that is great or that you should pay attention to

Synonym

- necessary

Antonym

- unimportant

Examples

- My grandfather's 70th birthday was an **important** event in our ______________ .

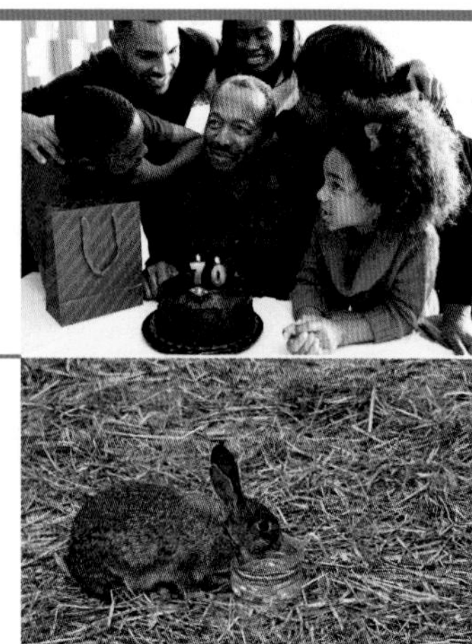

- It is very **important** to give your pet fresh ______________ every day.

TOOLKIT

Family

- **Noun:** importance

Word Partners

- very important
- important event

Examples

- To stay healthy, it is **very important** to eat fresh fruits and vegetables every day.
- Every year, our school celebrates several **important events**, such as President's Day in February.

 Try It

When you're getting dressed, it's very **important** to put on your ______________ before you put on your coat or sweater.

VERBAL PRACTICE

Talk about it — **Discuss ideas with your partner, listen to classmates, and then write your favorite idea.**

Discuss
Listen
Write

1. My partner and I agree that it is very **important** to study for this week's ______________ test.

2. For some third-graders, ______________ is the most **important** event of the year.

important
adjective

WRITING PRACTICE

Collaborate
Discuss
Listen
Agree
Write

Discuss ideas with your partner and agree on the best words to complete the frame.

One ________________ chore children can do to help before dinner is to ________________.

Our Turn
Discuss
Listen
Write

Read the prompt. Work with the teacher to complete the frames. Write a thoughtful response that includes an example.

PROMPT: What can you do to help your family remember an important school event?

To help my family remember an ________________ school event, I can post a note about it. For example, I can put a note on the ________________ in the kitchen or keep a reminder in my school ________________.

Be an Academic Author
Write
Discuss
Listen

Read the prompt and complete the frames. Strengthen your response with a reason.

PROMPT: What important behaviors can third-graders teach younger children?

Two ________________ behaviors third-graders can teach younger children are to be kind and ________________. The reason it is important for young ________________ to learn how to be kind is because it will help them make friends.

Construct a Response
Read
Discuss
Listen

Read the prompt and write a thoughtful response. Strengthen your response with a reason.

PROMPT: What is one important classroom rule that all students should remember?

____

____

____

grammar tip

Use the modal verb, or **helping verb**, ***can*** to show someone is able to do something. When you use ***can***, add a verb in the base form.

EXAMPLE: My sister **can skateboard** and **rollerblade** better than my brother.

topic

noun

Say it: top • ic

 ***Write it:*** ______________ ***Write it again:*** ______________

 ______________

TOOLKIT

Meaning

a thing that you talk, write, or read about

Synonym

- subject

Examples

- At the assembly, the vet's **topic** was what to ________ our class guinea pig.

- During our social studies lesson, the **topic** of our discussion was ________ .

Forms

- **Singular:** topic
- **Plural:** topics

Word Partners	Examples
• main topic of	• Bicycle safety was the **main topic of** the police officer's presentation.
• topic of our discussion	• During lunch, the **topic of our discussion** was our favorite fruit.

 **Try It**

When I read about animals, my favorite **topic** is ______________ .

VERBAL PRACTICE

Talk about it

Discuss
Listen
Write

Discuss ideas with your partner, listen to classmates, and then write your favorite idea.

1. At the science museum, the main **topic** of one amazing display was how to build (a/an) ______________ ______________ .

2. The **topic** of our class discussion was careers, so our teacher invited (a/an) ______________ ______________ to visit our class.

topic

noun

WRITING PRACTICE

Collaborate

Discuss
Listen
Agree
Write

Discuss ideas with your partner and agree on the best words to complete the frame.

Sometimes my partner and I can't agree on a ______________________ for our report. However, today we agreed to write about ______________________.

Our Turn

Discuss
Listen
Write

Read the prompt. Work with the teacher to complete the frames. Write a thoughtful response that includes an experience.

PROMPT: What was a recent topic of discussion during social studies? What did you enjoy learning about?

During a recent social studies lesson, the ______________________ of our discussion was ______________________. Personally, I enjoyed learning about the ______________________.

Be an Academic Author

Write
Discuss
Listen

Read the prompt and complete the frames. Strengthen your response with an example.

PROMPT: After you choose a topic for a report, what do you usually do next?

After I choose a ______________________ for a report, I usually find ways to ______________________ more about it. For example, I can talk to my teacher, search online, or find (a/an) __________ ______________________ in the library.

Construct a Response

Read
Discuss
Listen

Read the prompt and write a thoughtful response. Strengthen your response with an example.

PROMPT: What is one topic you and your best friend usually discuss on the weekends?

____

____

____

grammar tip

An adverb that tells how many times something happens can go before or after a verb. The adverbs ***always***, ***usually***, ***sometimes***, ***often***, and ***never*** can go before or after a verb.

EXAMPLE: When I get home from school, I **usually** eat a snack and then do my homework.

detail

noun

Say it: de • tail

 ***Write it:*** ______________ ***Write it again:*** ______________

 ______________

TOOLKIT

Meaning

a piece of information about something

Synonyms

- piece; part

Examples

- Using a magnifying glass, you can see every **detail** on a ______________.

- When my uncle ______________ his car, he pays attention to every **detail**.

Forms

- **Singular:** detail
- **Plural:** details

Family

- **Adjective:** detailed

Word Partners

- important detail
- describe ________ in detail

Examples

- The picture of President Lincoln is an **important detail** on a penny.
- In his report, my friend **described the book in detail.**

 **Try It**

One important **detail** to remember when you study for a test is to ______________ your notes.

VERBAL PRACTICE

Talk about it

Discuss
Listen
Write

Discuss ideas with your partner, listen to classmates, and then write your favorite idea.

1. Before we finished writing our story, we argued about which **details** were most ______________.

2. We can still describe in **detail** what happened during last year's class party to celebrate ______________.

WRITING PRACTICE

Collaborate

Discuss
Listen
Agree
Write

Discuss ideas with your partner and agree on the best words to complete the frame.

The detective asked the witnesses to describe in ______________________ what happened before they noticed that the ______________________ was missing.

Our Turn

Discuss
Listen
Write

Read the prompt. Work with the teacher to complete the frames. Write a thoughtful response that includes an example.

PROMPT: Why should you include several of details in any story you write?

Including several ______________________ can make any story more ______________________. For example, using many adjectives to describe people and ______________________ will make everyone want to read your stories.

Be an Academic Author

Write
Discuss
Listen

Read the prompt and complete the frames. Strengthen your response with an experience.

PROMPT: Describe in detail what happened when you tasted a food you did not like.

I remember in ______________________ how I felt the first time I tasted ______________________. My throat tightened, and I wanted to ______________________ to get the taste out of my mouth.

Construct a Response

Read
Discuss
Listen

Read the prompt and write a thoughtful response. Strengthen your response with an experience.

PROMPT: What is your favorite activity at recess? Include one important detail about it.

____

____

____

grammar tip

A **past-tense verb** describes an action that already happened. To write the past tense, add *-ed* to the end of a verb.

EXAMPLE: Last week, I **visited** my grandmother in Iowa. She **seemed** glad to see me.

information

noun

Say it: in • for • **ma** • tion

 ***Write it:*** ______________ ***Write it again:*** ______________

____

TOOLKIT

Meaning

details about something or someone

Synonym

- news

Examples

- The librarian showed me how to ______________ **information** online about turtles.

- The menu included **information** about healthy ______________ items.

Forms

- **Singular:** information

Family

- **Adjective:** informational

Word Partners

- piece of information
- contains information about

Examples

- One surprising **piece of information** about monkeys is that they can swim.
- An article in today's newspaper **contains information about** our school play.

 **Try It**

My cousin e-mailed **information** about the ______________ we planned to attend.

VERBAL PRACTICE

Talk about it

Discuss
Listen
Write

Discuss ideas with your partner, listen to classmates, and then write your favorite idea.

1. In order to get permission to go on a field trip to the zoo, we'll need to share **information** with our ______________.

2. We can help new students by giving them **information** about how to find the ______________.

WRITING PRACTICE

Collaborate

Discuss
Listen
Agree
Write

Discuss ideas with your partner and agree on the best words to complete the frame.

To get a library card, you need to provide ______________________________

about yourself, such as your ______________________________.

Our Turn

Discuss
Listen
Write

Read the prompt. Work with the teacher to complete the frames. Write a thoughtful response that includes a reason.

PROMPT: Why is it important to read the information provided on food labels?

A food label contains ______________________________ about key

ingredients. It is important to read the label to find out if the food contains any

______________________________ because those ingredients can be very

______________________________ for people with health problems.

Be an Academic Author

Write
Discuss
Listen

Read the prompt and complete the frames. Strengthen your response with an example.

PROMPT: What type of helpful information can a Web site provide about bad weather?

A Web site can provide helpful ______________________________

about how to be prepared for bad weather. For example, a weather Web page might

recommend that you take (a/an) ______________________________

______________________________ if rain is expected.

Construct a Response

Read
Discuss
Listen

Read the prompt and write a thoughtful response. Strengthen your response with an example.

PROMPT: What kind of information do you need before you begin playing a new game?

____

____

____

grammar tip

Noncount nouns name things that cannot be counted. Noncount nouns have the same form for "one" or "more than one." Do **not** add **-s** to a noncount noun to make it plural.

EXAMPLE: To make pancakes for 300 **people**, you need a lot of **flour**, **sugar**, and **water**.

fact

noun

Say it: fact

 **Write it:** ______________ **Write it again:** ______________

 ______________

TOOLKIT

Meaning

information that is true

Examples

- An important **fact** about __________ is that they lived long ago.

- One interesting **fact** about a cheetah is that it can __________ faster than any other four-legged animal.

Forms

- **Singular:** fact
- **Plural:** facts

Family

- **Adjective:** factual

Word Partners

- important fact
- interesting fact

Examples

- An **important fact** to remember is that chocolate can be very dangerous for dogs.
- An **interesting fact** about Alaska is that the sun shines until 9:00 or 10:00 at night during the summer.

 **Try It**

My report about the state of ______________ contains many important **facts**.

VERBAL PRACTICE

Talk about it **Discuss ideas with your partner, listen to classmates, and then write your favorite idea.**

Discuss
Listen
Write

1. The **fact** that I got an A on my ______________ test was a surprise.

2. Our school is proud of the **fact** that our ______________ team won every game last year.

fact

noun

WRITING PRACTICE

Collaborate

Discuss
Listen
Agree
Write

Discuss ideas with your partner and agree on the best words to complete the frame.

It is a ______________________ that some animals can change their appearance to protect themselves from danger. For example, a chameleon changes color to match its environment so other animals won't ______________________ it.

Our Turn

Discuss
Listen
Write

Read the prompt. Work with the teacher to complete the frames. Write a thoughtful response that includes a reason.

PROMPT: **What is one important fact to remember when you ride your bike?**

One important ______________________ to remember when you ride your bike is to ______________________. This will help protect your ______________________.

Be an Academic Author

Write
Discuss
Listen

Read the prompt and complete the frames. Strengthen your response with a reason.

PROMPT: **Imagine that you walked into your classroom and noticed: 1) the window was open; 2) the garbage was overturned; 3) pawprints led to and from the window. What do these important facts suggest to you?**

These important ______________________ suggest that (a/an) ______________________ might have entered the classroom. I know this because this animal often loves to find ______________________ in interesting places.

Construct a Response

Read
Discuss
Listen

Read the prompt and write a thoughtful response. Strengthen your response with a reason.

PROMPT: **What are two interesting facts about yourself to share with a new friend?**

____

____

____

grammar tip

The **preposition *to*** needs to be followed by a base verb.

EXAMPLE: My family likes **to visit** my grandparents in December.

example

noun

Say it: ex • **am** • ple

 **Write it:** ________________ **Write it again:** ________________

 ________________

TOOLKIT

Meaning

an idea that you use to show what you mean when talking or writing

Examples

- These parrots are **examples** of tropical ________.
- Putting ________ in a garbage container is an **example** of how you can help save the planet.

Forms

- **Singular:** example
- **Plural:** examples

Word Partners	Examples
• For example,	• Our science book includes several informational pictures. **For example**, Unit 1 has many photos of a shark's teeth and jaw, which explain its dangerous bite.
• ______ is an example of ______	• **A donut is an example of a food** that contains a lot of sugar and fat.

 **Try It**

My friend is an **example** of a happy, ________________ person.

VERBAL PRACTICE

Talk about it **Discuss ideas with your partner, listen to classmates, and then write your favorite idea.**

Discuss
Listen
Write

1. Two **examples** of words that start with the prefix *un-* are *unfit* and

________________________________.

2. My friends and I enjoy the same school subjects. For **example**, we all like math and ________________________.

WRITING PRACTICE

Collaborate

Discuss
Listen
Agree
Write

Discuss ideas with your partner and agree on the best words to complete the frame.

Dominos and checkers are ______________________ of the kinds of games my ______________________ likes to play on a rainy day.

Our Turn

Discuss
Listen
Write

Read the prompt. Work with the teacher to complete the frames. Write a thoughtful response that includes a reason.

PROMPT: What is one example of a book you would like to recommend?

One ______________________ of a book I would recommend is ______________________. I would recommend this book because it contains many ______________________ events.

Be an Academic Author

Write
Discuss
Listen

Read the prompt and complete the frames. Strengthen your response with a reason.

PROMPT: Many animals make excellent pets. What is one example?

One ______________________ of an excellent pet is a furry ______________________. This animal is a good pet because it likes to be with people and is easy to ______________________.

Construct a Response

Read
Discuss
Listen

Read the prompt and write a thoughtful response. Strengthen your response with a reason.

PROMPT: What is one example of a healthy after-school snack that you like to eat?

____

____

____

____

grammar tip

The preposition ***to*** needs to be followed by a base verb.

EXAMPLE: It is important **to eat** fruit and vegetables every day.

important

SMART START

REVIEW: event *noun*

DAY 1

One big ______________________ I'm looking forward to is the ______________________ fair in the spring. ☐ ☐

important *adjective*

DAY 2

It is ______________________ to have a ______________________ attitude at school. ☐ ☐

DAY 3

When you cross a street, one ______________________ rule is to ______________________. ☐ ☐

DAY 4

Fresh vegetables, such as ______________________, are ______________________ because they can help build strong bones and teeth. ☐ ☐

DAY 5

An ______________________ event in my life was the day I learned how to ______________________. ☐ ☐

TOTAL ☐

SMART START

REVIEW: important *adjective*

DAY 1

Our teacher says that we should include ______________ pictures, maps, or diagrams to ______________ the events in our stories. ☐ ☐

topic *noun*

DAY 2

The main ______________ of the coach's talk was how to ______________ the ball correctly. ☐ ☐

DAY 3

During reading period, our class usually discusses three ______________. We talk about the events, the setting, and what the character ______________. ☐ ☐

DAY 4

At dinner, our parents/guardians encourage us to discuss several pleasant ______________, such as what we learned at school and what we did at recess. They do not want us to use bad language or ______________. ☐ ☐

DAY 5

When we plan a ______________ party, it is important to discuss two ______________: games we will play and foods we will eat. ☐ ☐

TOTAL

detail

REVIEW: topic ***noun***

DAY 1

One _______________ I like to discuss with my parents/guardian is our next vacation. We talk about where we will go and what we plan to _______________.

detail ***noun***

DAY 2

If you look closely, you can see several _______________ in a single plant. For example, you can see more than one color and several different _______________.

DAY 3

When I write stories about my friends, I like to include as many _______________ as possible. This makes my stories more _______________.

DAY 4

When people get to know me, the single _______________ that surprises people most is my ability to _______________ well.

DAY 5

Every _______________ in a recipe is important. Leaving out an ingredient can make the food taste _______________ instead of delicious.

TOTAL

SMART START

REVIEW: detail *noun*

DAY 1

I will remember forever every single ______________________

in my favorite ______________________.

information *noun*

DAY 2

A good book report provides specific ______________________,

such as the author's name and why you ______________________

the story.

DAY 3

The ______________________ the magazine provided about

dinosaurs was so ______________________

I just had to tell my friend about it.

DAY 4

The weather report provided important ______________________

about the upcoming ______________________.

DAY 5

During flu season, the ______________________ provided

important ______________________ about how to stay healthy.

TOTAL

fact

REVIEW: information *noun*

DAY 1

To get ______________________________

for your report, you should use reliable sources, such as (a/an) ______________ ☐

______________________________ . ☐

fact *noun*

DAY 2

One important ______________________ about our school is ☐

that ______________________ students attend classes here. ☐

DAY 3

Yesterday, our teacher announced a surprising ______________ .

The school year will begin in the month of ______________ ☐

next year. ☐

DAY 4

Two interesting ______________________________

about the solar system are that the planets always orbit around the Sun, but ☐

______________________ have been found only on Earth. ☐

DAY 5

An interesting ______________________________

is that some birds and bees have ______________________ ☐

color vision and can see colors that people can't see. ☐

TOTAL

SMART START

REVIEW: fact *noun*

DAY 1

An important ______________________

about bees is that they ______________________.

example *noun*

DAY 2

I like to play games with my ______________________

after school. For ______________________,

I play video games almost every day.

DAY 3

The fruits we eat come from plants. Two ______________________

are berries that come from bushes and ______________________

that come from trees.

DAY 4

Big storms can cause a lot of damage to ______________________.

Tornadoes and hurricanes are ______________________ of big storms.

DAY 5

Our school celebrates holidays in different ways. For ______________________,

we have a costume contest for Halloween and a big party for

______________________.

TOTAL

Toolkit Unit 3 | Cause and Effect

Cause and Effect

A **cause** makes something happen.

Ask yourself, "Why did it happen?"

To find the **cause**, look for clue words such as *since, because,* and *reason.*

An **effect** is what happens.

Ask yourself, "What happened?"

To find the **effect**, look for clue words such as *so, as a result,* and *therefore.*

Find It **Read the sentences. Label the cause and the effect.**

I didn't feel well. → I stayed home from school.

I didn't feel well ***so*** I stayed home from school.

Cause ______ Effect ______

It is the start of fall. → The leaves on the trees are turning yellow and orange.

The leaves on the trees are turning yellow and orange ***because*** it is the start of fall.

______ ______

Try It **Complete the sentences. Then label the cause and the effect in each sentence.**

My cousin hurt her toe so she couldn't play in the ______ game.

______ ______

RATE WORD KNOWLEDGE

Circle the number that shows your knowledge of the words you'll use to speak and write about cause and effect.

RATE IT

BEFORE	3rd Grade	AFTER	4th Grade	5th Grade
1 2 3 4	**cause**	1 2 3 4	result	impact
1 2 3 4	**effect**	1 2 3 4	consequence	factor
1 2 3 4	**problem**	1 2 3 4	affect	result
1 2 3 4	**solution**	1 2 3 4	lead	alter
1 2 3 4	**happen**	1 2 3 4	occur	influence
1 2 3 4	**change**	1 2 3 4	reaction	outcome

DISCUSSION GUIDE

- Form groups of four.
- Assign letters to each person.
- Each group member takes a turn leading a discussion.
- Prepare to report about one word.

A B
D C

DISCUSS WORDS

Discuss how well you know the third grade words. Then, report to the class how you rated each word.

GROUP LEADER **Ask**

So, ______ (NAME) what do you know about the word ______ ?

GROUP MEMBERS **Discuss**

1 = I **have never seen or heard** the word ______ . I need to learn what it means.

2 = I **have seen or heard** the word ______ , but I need to learn the meaning.

3 = I'm **familiar** with the word ______ . I think it means ______ .

4 = I **know** the word ______ . It means ______ .

REPORTER **Report Word Knowledge**

Our group gave the word ______ a rating of ______ .

SET A GOAL AND REFLECT

First, set a vocabulary goal for this unit by selecting at least two words that you plan to thoroughly learn. At the end of the unit, return to this page and write a reflection about one word you have mastered.

GOAL

During this unit I plan to thoroughly learn the words ______ and ______ . Increasing my word knowledge will help me speak and write effectively about Cause and ______ .

REFLECTION

As a result of this unit, I feel most confident about the word ______ . This is my model sentence: ______ ______ .

cause

noun

Say it: cause

 ***Write it:*** ___________ ***Write it again:*** ___________

 ___________

TOOLKIT

Meaning
something that makes another thing happen

Synonym
- reason

Antonym
- effect

Examples
- Pollen on the flowers was the main **cause** of my cousin's ___________.
- The dog was the **cause** of the huge ___________ in the house.

Forms
- **Singular:** cause
- **Plural:** causes

Family
- **Verb:** cause

Word Partners	Examples
• a/the cause of _____	• The detectives tried to find **the cause of** the fire at the toy store.
• the main cause of _____	• The dentist said that not brushing my teeth twice a day was **the main cause of** my cavities.

 **Try It**

My friends wanted to know the **cause** of my absence from ___________ yesterday.

VERBAL PRACTICE

Talk about it — **Discuss ideas with your partner, listen to classmates, and then write your favorite idea.**

Discuss
Listen
Write

1. We decided to write a report about the main **cause** of litter on our ___________ ___________.

2. Our substitute teacher went into the hallway to find the **cause** of the ___________ noise.

WRITING PRACTICE

Collaborate
Discuss
Listen
Agree
Write

Discuss ideas with your partner and agree on the best words to complete the frame.

Falling is a common ______________________ of accidents. This is why caring teachers tell students to be careful on the ______________________.

Our Turn
Discuss
Listen
Write

Read the prompt. Work with the teacher to complete the frames. Write a thoughtful response that includes an example.

PROMPT: Some children are afraid of the dark. What is the main cause of their fear?

The main ______________________ of fear of the dark among young children is usually due to a fear of the unknown. When a room is too dark to see, some children imagine things, such as ______________________.

Be an Academic Author
Write
Discuss
Listen

Read the prompt and complete the frames. Strengthen your response with a reason.

PROMPT: Imagine that the principal announced that in the mornings students must stay on the playground until the bell rings. What do you think might be the main cause for this decision?

I think the main ______________ for the principal's decision might be because he thought the ______________ were spending too much time inside. Our principal wants students to ______________ in the fresh air every morning.

Construct a Response
Read
Discuss
Listen

Read the prompt and write a thoughtful response. Strengthen your response with a reason.

PROMPT: Imagine that your class received free tickets to a movie from the principal. What could have been the cause of this gift?

____

____

____

grammar tip

Adjectives are always singular even if they describe a plural noun. Do not add **-s** to adjectives that describe plural nouns.

EXAMPLE: The **tall** giraffe ate the **tender green** leaves at the top of the tree.

effect

noun

Say it: ef • fect

 ***Write it:*** ______________________ ***Write it again:*** ______________________

 ______________________

TOOLKIT

Meaning

a change that is caused by something or is the result of something

Synonym

- result

Antonym

- cause

Examples

- The visit from the therapy ____________ had a positive **effect** on my cousin's health.

- One **effect** of too much time in the sun can be a painful ______________________.

Forms

- **Singular:** effect
- **Plural:** effects

Family

- **Verb:** effect

Word Partners

- have a positive/negative effect on _____ (someone/something)
- the effect(s) of _____ on _____

Examples

- A cheerful teacher can **have a positive effect on** your attitude about school.
- **The effect of fudge sauce on** my ice cream was a great improvement in the taste of my sundae.

 **Try It**

I will never forget the **effect** of seeing my lost ______________________ again.

VERBAL PRACTICE

Talk about it — Discuss, Listen, Write

Discuss ideas with your partner, listen to classmates, and then write your favorite idea.

1. Getting a new pet had a positive **effect** on our family because now we spend more time together playing with the ______________________.
2. The cold and rainy weather last week had a negative **effect** on our ______________________ team's ability to win the game.

WRITING PRACTICE

Collaborate
Discuss
Listen
Agree
Write

Discuss ideas with your partner and agree on the best words to complete the frames.

Breathing in pollen or dust can have a negative ______________________ on people with allergies. It often makes them ______________________.

Our Turn
Discuss
Listen
Write

Read the prompt. Work with the teacher to complete the frames. Write a thoughtful response that includes an example.

PROMPT: **What is one possible effect that you hope for when you play four square?**

One possible ______________________ that I hope for when I play four square is a winning move. For example, I try to ______________________ the ball in the far corner so my opponent can't ______________________ it.

Be an Academic Author
Write
Discuss
Listen

Read the prompt and complete the frames. Strengthen your response with a reason.

PROMPT: **What is one kind of music that can have a positive effect on your mood?**

One kind of music that can have a positive ______________________ on my mood is ______________________ music because it makes me feel ______________________.

Construct a Response
Read
Discuss
Listen

Read the prompt and write a thoughtful response. Strengthen your response with a reason.

PROMPT: **If you are having a bad day, what effect can a note from a friend have on you?**

____

____

____

grammar tip

Use the **modal verb**, or **helping verb**, ***can*** to show that something is possible. When you use ***can***, add a verb in the base form.

EXAMPLE: A cloudy day **can make** you feel sad, but a sunny day **can make** you feel happy.

problem

noun

Say it: prob • lem

Write it: ______________ ***Write it again:*** ______________

 ______________

TOOLKIT

Meaning	Examples	
a difficult situation **Synonyms** • trouble; difficulty **Antonym** • solution	• My dad helped me fix the **problem** I had with my ______________ .	
	• The main **problem** my family is experiencing is that my new baby sister ______________ at night.	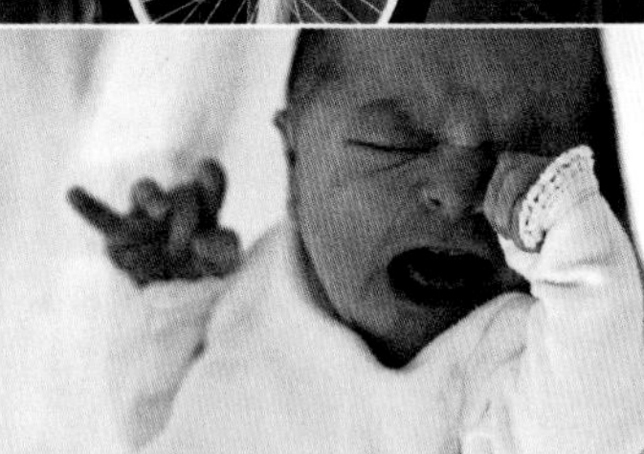

Forms

- **Singular:** problem
- **Plural:** problems

Word Partners	Examples
• a/the main problem	• I like stories in which **the main problem** is a funny disagreement between two friends.
• deal with a/the problem	• Some schools have to **deal with the problem** of bullying.

 **Try It**

When I have a **problem** at school, I like to talk it over with my ______________ .

VERBAL PRACTICE

Talk about it — Discuss / Listen / Write

Discuss ideas with your partner, listen to classmates, and then write your favorite idea.

1. My cousin and I got lost at the ______________ , so we found a security guard who helped us deal with the **problem**.
2. When our friend had a **problem** with her rollerblades, we found (a/an) ______________ ______________ that explained how to fix them.

WRITING PRACTICE

Collaborate

Discuss
Listen
Agree
Write

Discuss ideas with your partner and agree on the best words to complete the frame.

Sometimes my mom has a ______________________________ getting her cell phone to work. She becomes irritated when she can't get important ______________________________ from her boss.

Our Turn

Discuss
Listen
Write

Read the prompt. Work with the teacher to complete the frames. Write a thoughtful response that includes a reason.

PROMPT: Sometimes partners interrupt each other. How can you solve this problem?

One way to solve this ______________________________ is to remind Partner A to wait until Partner B is done speaking. That way, both ______________________________ will have a chance to share their excellent ______________________________.

Be an Academic Author

Write
Discuss
Listen

Read the prompt and complete the frames. Strengthen your response with a reason.

PROMPT: What is one problem your class needs to solve before going on a field trip?

One ______________________________ that our class needs to solve is what to do with our lunches when we go on a field trip to the ______________________________.

My suggestion is to put the lunches in (a/an) ______________________________ ______________________________ to keep them safe and cool until it's time to eat.

Construct a Response

Read
Discuss
Listen

Read the prompt and write a thoughtful response. Strengthen your response with a reason.

PROMPT: If you are served food that you don't like, how can you solve the problem?

____

____

____

grammar tip

Adjectives are always singular even if they describe a plural noun. Do not add **-s** to adjectives that describe plural nouns.

EXAMPLE: The **cute**, **little** puppies enjoyed their trip to the **huge** park.

solution

noun

Say it: so • **lu** • tion

 ***Write it:*** ____________________ ***Write it again:*** ____________________

 ____________________

TOOLKIT

Meaning

a way to solve a problem

Synonym

- answer

Antonym

- problem

Examples

- When our cafeteria was closed for repairs, my **solution** was to bring my __________.

- When our dog had too many __________, our **solution** was to give some away.

Forms

- **Singular:** solution
- **Plural:** solutions

Word Partners

- good solution
- solution to a/the problem

Examples

- A **good solution** to the problem of litter on the playground is to have each class take turns picking up after lunch.
- Scientists are working hard to find a **solution to the problem** of cancer.

 **Try It**

After too many students lined up at the pencil sharpener, my teacher's **solution** was to allow only two ______________________________ to be in line at one time.

VERBAL PRACTICE

Talk about it **Discuss ideas with your partner, listen to classmates, and then write your favorite idea.**

Discuss
Listen
Write

1. At our house we used to run out of cereal and ____________________ often, so our **solution** was to put a family grocery list on the refrigerator.

2. After the party we had several ____________________ left, so our teacher's **solution** was to give the food to the local homeless shelter.

solution

noun

WRITING PRACTICE

Collaborate
Discuss
Listen
Agree
Write

Discuss ideas with your partner and agree on the best words to complete the frame.

You can find creative ______________________ to important problems, such as ______________________ and junk food by discussing them with students and teachers.

Our Turn
Discuss
Listen
Write

Read the prompt. Work with the teacher to complete the frames. Write a thoughtful response that includes a reason.

PROMPT: Imagine that your teacher is worried because books are always scattered around the reading corner. What would be a good solution to this problem?

A good ________________ to the problem of scattered books would be to have a student in charge of the reading corner. This way, the student would keep the books ________________ by putting them on the ________________ shelves.

Be an Academic Author
Write
Discuss
Listen

Read the prompt and complete the frames. Strengthen your response with an example.

PROMPT: Imagine that your dog ran away while your parents/guardians weren't home. What is a good solution to this problem?

If my dog ran away, a good ______________________ to this problem is to ask my ______________________ to help me search. For example, we could look in places where my dog likes to play or ______________________ .

Construct a Response
Read
Discuss
Listen

Read the prompt and write a thoughtful response. Strengthen your response with a reason.

PROMPT: Imagine this problem: You like to play games with your best friend, but your friend likes to watch TV most of the time. What can be a solution to this problem?

____

____

____

grammar tip

Use a **verb + *-ing*** after the **prepositions** ***by***, ***of***, and ***for***.

EXAMPLE: I can always get my baby brother to laugh **by making** a silly face.

happen

verb

Say it: hap • pen

Write it: ________________ ***Write it again:*** ________________

____

TOOLKIT

Meaning

to take place without being planned

Examples

- My friend was surprised about what **happened** at the end of the ________.

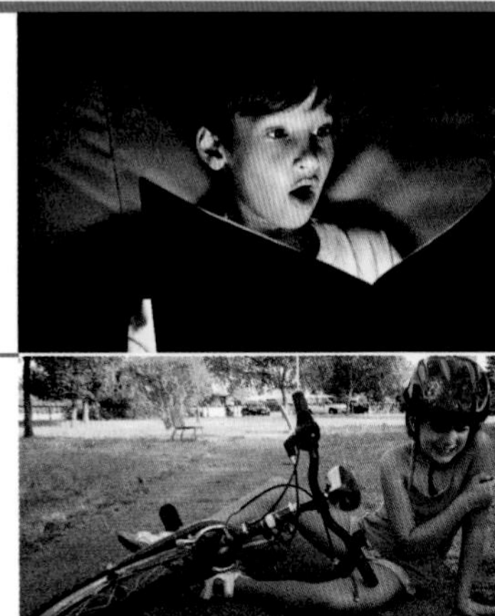

- My cousin's ________ accident **happened** last week.

Forms

- **Present:**
  they happen
  it happens
- **Past:** happened

Word Partners

- happen at _____
- happen(s) to _____ (someone/something)

Examples

- The fire drill **happened at lunch time**, so we had to leave our lunches and line up on the playground.
- I'm curious about what will **happen to the birds** in winter.

Try It

I don't remember how it **happened**, but I learned to ________________ when I was six.

VERBAL PRACTICE

Talk about it **Discuss ideas with your partner, listen to classmates, and then write your favorite idea.**

Discuss
Listen
Write

1. We couldn't believe what **happened** when it started to rain right in the middle of our ________________ yesterday.

2. The students are excited to see what might **happen** when the new ________________ arrives at our school next week.

happen

verb

WRITING PRACTICE

Collaborate
Discuss
Listen
Agree
Write

Discuss ideas with your partner and agree on the best words to complete the frame.

Several special events _______________ every year at our school. Our favorite event is the _______________.

Our Turn
Discuss
Listen
Write

Read the prompt. Work with the teacher to complete the frames. Write a thoughtful response that includes a reason.

PROMPT: **Why do some mistakes happen during tests and how can you avoid them?**

Mistakes sometimes _______________ during tests when you feel _______________ and aren't careful with your answers. A way to avoid mistakes is by taking your time and by _______________ questions carefully.

Be an Academic Author
Write
Discuss
Listen

Read the prompt and complete the frames. Strengthen your response with an example.

PROMPT: **How can you make sure fun things will happen at a party?**

To make sure fun things _______________ at a party, I can plan ahead. For example, I can plan to serve my friends' favorite snacks, such as _______________, and set up places to play _______________ games.

Construct a Response
Write
Discuss
Listen

Read the prompt and write a thoughtful response. Strengthen your response with a reason.

PROMPT: **Describe one thing that you wish would happen next summer.**

____

____

____

grammar tip

A **present tense verb** describes an action that is happening now, usually, sometimes, or never. If the subject of a sentence is *he, she, it*, add **-s** to the end of a verb.

EXAMPLE: Sometimes my friend **tells** me funny jokes, and I **laugh** until I cry.

change

verb

Say it: change

 ***Write it:*** ______________ ***Write it again:*** ______________

 ______________

TOOLKIT

Meaning

to become different; to make something different

Examples

- Before parent conferences, our teacher **changed** the ________ on the bulletin board.
- In the fall, the ________ on the trees and bushes **change** colors.

Forms

- **Present:**
  I/You/We/They happen
  He/She/It changes
- **Past:** changed

Family

- **Noun:** change

Word Partners

- change completely
- (rapidly/suddenly/slowly) change

Examples

- At night, the Ferris wheel **changes completely** to look like a glowing space ship.
- To protect itself from enemies, a chameleon **slowly changes** its color to match its environment.

 **Try It**

After school, I **changed** my mind and went to the ______________ instead of to the park.

VERBAL PRACTICE

Talk about it

Discuss
Listen
Write

Discuss ideas with your partner, listen to classmates, and then write your favorite idea.

1. Before we performed our ______________ for the parents, we had to **change** the chairs in the classroom.

2. When the cafeteria **changed** the lunch menu, everyone loved the new items, especially the ______________ soup.

change
verb

WRITING PRACTICE

Collaborate
Discuss
Listen
Agree
Write

Discuss ideas with your partner and agree on the best words to complete the frame.

After finding a great picture online we ______________________ the focus of our science report and wrote about ______________________ instead of tornadoes.

Our Turn
Discuss
Listen
Write

Read the prompt. Work with the teacher to complete the frames. Write a thoughtful response that includes a reason.
PROMPT: How does a caterpillar change during its lifetime?

A caterpillar ______________________ from a worm form into a butterfly form. After eating leaves, it attaches itself to a ______________________ of a tree and forms a cocoon. Next, it grows wings, and it ______________________ emerges as a butterfly.

Be an Academic Author
Write
Discuss
Listen

Read the prompt and complete the frames. Strengthen your response with an experience.
PROMPT: As you've gotten older, have your interests in movies changed?

My interests in movies keep ______________________ as I get older. In first grade I enjoyed movies about ______________________, but now I prefer movies about ______________________.

Construct a Response
Write
Discuss
Listen

Read the prompt and write a thoughtful response. Strengthen your response with an experience.
PROMPT: Have math assignments changed in third grade? What can you do now that you couldn't do in first or second grade?

____

____

____

grammar tip

A **past-tense verb** describes an action that already happened. For verbs that end in silent **e**, drop the final **e** before you add ***-ed***.

EXAMPLE: As soon as the new puppies **arrived**, I **raced** home to see them.

cause

REVIEW: example *noun*

DAY 1

My cat is a good ______________________ of a crazy pet because she climbs the curtains and ______________________ from chair to chair across the living room. ☐ ☐

cause *noun*

DAY 2

People say that one of the main ______________________ of happiness is getting plenty of time to ______________________. ☐ ☐

DAY 3

Eating too much ______________________ can be one ______________________ of a bad stomach ache. ☐ ☐

DAY 4

The main ______________________ of our class's good test grades is that we studied every ______________________. ☐ ☐

DAY 5

Everyone thought the enormous tree fell because it had too many ______________________, but the scientist said the real ______________________ was a weak root system. ☐ ☐

TOTAL

SMART START

REVIEW: cause *noun*

DAY 1

Our third-grade science textbook taught me that not eating enough fresh ______________________ could be one ______________________ of weak muscles.

effect *noun*

DAY 2

I like listening to songs by ______________________ because they have a positive ______________________ on my mood.

DAY 3

After watching the health program, I knew that one ______________________ of eating a lot of ______________________ could be cavities in my teeth.

DAY 4

Not getting enough exercise can have negative ______________________ on a pet's behavior. For example, if a ______________________ doesn't get enough exercise, it might feel bored and damage the furniture.

DAY 5

Too much sugar has a bizarre ______________________ on my friend. Sometimes (he/she) __________ ______________________ around at recess.

TOTAL

problem

REVIEW: effect *noun*

DAY 1

The most surprising ______________________________

of the sudden cold weather was the beautiful ice that decorated all the

______________________________ .

problem *noun*

DAY 2

My best friend and I sometimes have a ______________________________

agreeing on what to do during ______________________________ .

DAY 3

Last summer, we had a ______________________________ with flies,

so my father reminded everyone to close all the ______________________________

in our house.

DAY 4

During a school construction project, the big machines caused a

______________________________ during our visits to the library. So the librarian

tried to help us ______________________________ by playing soft music while we read.

DAY 5

To solve all the park's ______________________________ with

litter, my friends and I decided to make posters reminding people to put their

______________________________ in the cans.

TOTAL

REVIEW: problem *noun*

DAY 1

I decided to solve my ______________________ of too much homework by doing a few assignments as soon as I get home, and the rest after I finished my ______________________.

solution *noun*

DAY 2

When too many ______________________ wanted to play foursquare, we came up with a ______________________ by adding a new player whenever a player went "out."

DAY 3

A good ______________________ to low scores on a test is to study hard and get plenty of ______________________ before the next test.

DAY 4

If you miss the school bus, a good ______________________ is to call your ______________________ and ask for a ride.

DAY 5

Cutting up steak is too hard for my little brother, so a good ______________________ is to serve him ______________________ instead.

TOTAL

happen

REVIEW: solution *noun*

DAY 1

The best ______________________ for being late for the bus is to get up at ______________________ every morning.

happen *verb*

DAY 2

My family's best dinners usually ______________________ after Dad shops at the grocery store and buys chicken to make fajitas or ______________________.

DAY 3

I wonder what would ______________________ if I didn't go to school for ______________________ days in a row.

DAY 4

In places that have tough winter weather, one thing that ______________________ is that students often wear ______________________ when they go outside to play.

DAY 5

Last year when my youngest sister started ______________________, she was excited to tell me about what ______________________ every day at school.

TOTAL

REVIEW: happen *verb*

DAY 1

In August, a fire ______________ in the warehouse, so our class had to wait for new ______________ textbooks.

change *verb*

DAY 2

Recently, I ______________ the posters in my bedroom to show my favorite ______________ .

DAY 3

To improve the plans for our mom's birthday dinner last week, we ______________ the menu to include her favorite ______________ for dessert.

DAY 4

Yesterday, our coach ______________ the schedule for ______________ practice.

DAY 5

My feelings about writing ______________ when I learned to write in cursive because my writing looks more ______________ now.

TOTAL

Toolkit Unit 4 | Sequence

Sequence

Sequence is the order in which events happen. Use the signal words such as *first, next* and *last*, along with the Toolkit words in this unit to help you analyze, discuss, and write about the **sequence** of events.

Find It **Read the sentences. Determine the sequence and write 1st, 2nd, and 3rd to show the order in which the events happen.**

1. _____ On Tuesday, we enrolled Lucky in puppy training classes at the local pet shelter.
   _____ On Monday when I came home from school, I noticed that Lucky had chewed up our shoes!
   _____ Over the weekend, we got a new puppy named Lucky.

Try It **Show the sequence by describing what you might do after the first step.**

1. To make a hamburger, first, place the hamburger patty on one side of a bun.
2. Next, you can add condiments, such as ketchup and ______________________.
3. Finally, put the other bun on top and get ready to ______________________ your delicious hamburger!

RATE WORD KNOWLEDGE

Circle the number that shows your knowledge of the words you'll use to speak and write about sequence.

RATE IT

BEFORE	3rd Grade	AFTER	4th Grade	5th Grade
1 2 3 4	**order**	1 2 3 4	process	initially
1 2 3 4	**next**	1 2 3 4	final	previously
1 2 3 4	**before**	1 2 3 4	afterward	subsequently
1 2 3 4	**after**	1 2 3 4	following	eventually
1 2 3 4	**finally**	1 2 3 4	previous	ultimately
1 2 3 4	**following**	1 2 3 4	prior	preceding

DISCUSSION GUIDE

- Form groups of four.
- Assign letters to each person. Ⓐ Ⓑ Ⓓ Ⓒ
- Each group member takes a turn leading a discussion.
- Prepare to report about one word.

DISCUSS WORDS

Discuss how well you know the third grade words. Then, report to the class how you rated each word.

GROUP LEADER **Ask**

So, ______ (NAME) what do you know about the word ______ ?

GROUP MEMBERS **Discuss**

1 = I **have never seen or heard** the word ______ . I need to learn what it means.

2 = I **have seen or heard** the word ______ , but I need to learn the meaning.

3 = I'm **familiar** with the word ______ . I think it means ______ .

4 = I **know** the word ______ . It means ______ .

REPORTER **Report Word Knowledge**

Our group gave the word ______ a rating of ______ .

SET A GOAL AND REFLECT

First, set a vocabulary goal for this unit by selecting at least two words that you plan to thoroughly learn. At the end of the unit, return to this page and write a reflection about one word you have mastered.

GOAL

During this unit I plan to thoroughly learn the words ______ and ______ . Increasing my word knowledge will help me speak and write effectively about ______ .

REFLECTION

As a result of this unit, I feel most confident about the word ______ . This is my model sentence: ______ ______ .

order

noun

Say it: or • der

 ***Write it:*** ______________________ ***Write it again:*** ______________________

 ______________________

TOOLKIT

Meaning

the way that you arrange things, such as showing what goes first, second, third, etc.

Synonym

- sequence

Examples

- The students lined up in a special **order** to get on the __________ for the field trip.
- Our librarian arranges the __________ in alphabetical **order** on the shelves.

Forms

Family

- **Adjective:** orderly

Word Partners

- the correct order
- arrange (things, names, events) in (numerical, alphabetical) order

Examples

- One way to practice spelling new words is to write the letters in **the correct order** several times.
- My friend always **arranges the cards in numerical order** before he puts the deck away.

 **Try It**

I like to keep all the ______________________ in my drawer in **order** by color.

VERBAL PRACTICE

Talk about it **Discuss ideas with your partner, listen to classmates, and then write your favorite idea.**

Discuss
Listen
Write

1. Some elementary school teachers ask students to write their names on their ______________________ in this **order**: first name, then last name.

2. When I pack for a sleep-over, I organize my suitcase in this **order**: my ______________________ on the bottom and my toothbrush near the top.

WRITING PRACTICE

Collaborate

Discuss
Listen
Agree
Write

Discuss ideas with your partner and agree on the best words to complete the frame.

If we could arrange ice cream flavors in ______________________ of favorites, the flavor last on the list would be ______________________.

Our Turn

Discuss
Listen
Write

Read the prompt. Work with the teacher to complete the frames. Write a thoughtful response that includes an example.

PROMPT: In what order could you arrange people for a family photo?

For a family photo, I could arrange people in ______________________ by age. For example, the grandparents and older ______________________ could stand in back, and the younger ______________________ could sit in the front.

Be an Academic Author

Write
Discuss
Listen

Read the prompt and complete the frames. Strengthen your response with a reason.

PROMPT: What is the correct order to make a peanut butter and jelly sandwich?

Follow these steps in the correct ______________________ to make a perfect peanut butter and jelly sandwich: First, spread peanut butter on one slice of bread. Next, spread strawberry or ______________________ jelly on another slice of bread. Finally, ______________________ the slices together and eat your delicious sandwich!

Construct a Response

Read
Discuss
Listen

Read the prompt and write a thoughtful response. Strengthen your response with a reason.

PROMPT: In what order would you pack three special things to send to a cousin far away? Why is this order important?

____

____

____

grammar tip

Use the **modal verb**, or **helping verb**, ***could*** to show that something might be possible. When you use could, add a verb in the base form.

EXAMPLE: To invite friends to a party, you ***could*** send the invitations by e-mail.

next

adjective

Say it: next

 ***Write it:*** ______________________ ***Write it again:*** ______________________

 ______________________

TOOLKIT

Meaning

coming after this time, event, or step

Examples

- My sisters took the escalator to the **next** ____________ of the mall.

- My best friend is the **next** ____________ in line for the bus.

Forms

Family

- **Adverb:** next

Word Partners

- the next ____________ (time: day/morning/year)
- the next ____________ (thing: step/flight/question/etc.)

Examples

- During their last practice, the players were really thirsty. So **the next morning** the soccer coach brought plenty of water to practice.
- After we wash the dog, **the next step** is to dry him off before he goes back into the house.

 **Try It**

At the beginning of the school year, most students are excited about the new ______________________________ they will meet in the **next** few days.

VERBAL PRACTICE

Talk about it

Discuss
Listen
Write

Discuss ideas with your partner, listen to classmates, and then write your favorite idea.

1. After my neighbors moved away, I hoped that the **next** family to move in would have a ______________________________ my age.

2. My cousin played soccer all day, then he fell asleep before dinner. The **next** day he felt ______________________________.

WRITING PRACTICE

Collaborate
Discuss
Listen
Agree
Write

Discuss ideas with your partner and agree on the best words to complete the frame.

When a small ________________ saw a large hawk flying overhead, it escaped to a high branch on the ________________ tree.

Our Turn
Discuss
Listen
Write

Read the prompt. Work with the teacher to complete the frames. Write a thoughtful response that includes an experience.

PROMPT: After your teacher takes attendance, what are the next tasks to accomplish?

After our teacher takes attendance, the ________________ task is to review the calendar. After that, it's time for ________________.

Following these tasks in the same order each day helps us know what to ________________ during the school day.

Be an Academic Author
Write
Discuss
Listen

Read the prompt and complete the frames. Strengthen your response with an experience.

PROMPT: You probably have a bedtime routine. After you brush your teeth, what do you do next?

After I brush my teeth, the ________________ thing I do is ________________.

This bedtime routine helps me ________________ at night.

Construct a Response
Read
Discuss
Listen

Read the prompt and write a thoughtful response. Strengthen your response with a reason.

PROMPT: Describe a location you'd like to visit next summer. Why would you enjoy it?

____

____

____

grammar tip

A **common noun** names a person, place, thing, or idea. Singular nouns name one person, place, thing, or idea. The words *a, an,* and *the* often appear before a singular noun.

EXAMPLE: The scary old **house** had a **door** that creaked and the **yard** was full of **weeds**.

before

preposition

Say it: be • fore

 ***Write it:*** ______________ ***Write it again:*** ______________

____

TOOLKIT

Meaning

coming earlier than or ahead of someone or something

Antonym

- after

Synonym

- earlier

Examples

- It is important to wash your ______________ thoroughly **before** every meal.

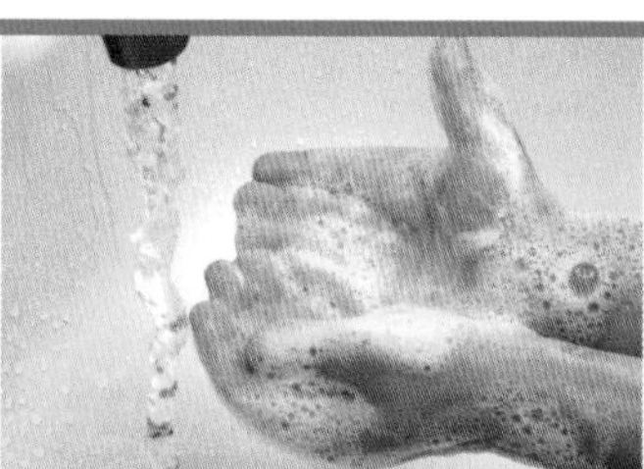

- The farmers feed the baby ______________ **before** 5:00 a.m. every day.

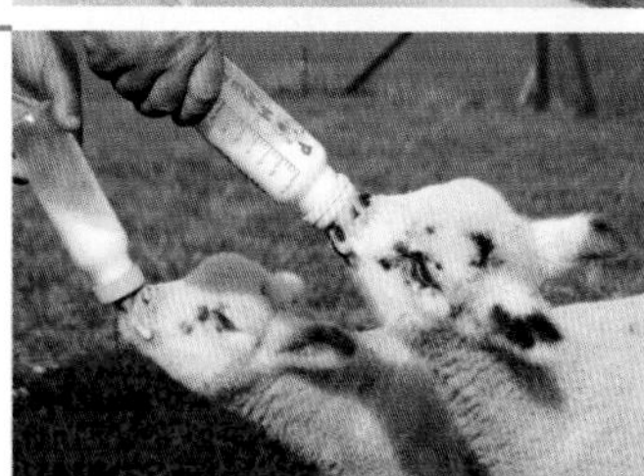

Forms

Family

Word Partners

- (do something) before ______ (an activity, e.g., school, breakfast, bed)
- the (time/week/day) before ______

Examples

- I always polish my trumpet **before band practice**.
- My grandmother came to visit me **the day before yesterday**.

 **Try It**

I'm usually at the bus stop at least ______________ minutes **before** the eight o'clock bus.

VERBAL PRACTICE

Talk about it

Discuss
Listen
Write

Discuss ideas with your partner, listen to classmates, and then write your favorite idea.

1. We finished taking the ______________ test just **before** the lunch bell.

2. Since the boys were quietest, the teacher asked the them to line up to go into the ______________ **before** the girls.

before

preposition

WRITING PRACTICE

Collaborate

Discuss
Listen
Agree
Write

Discuss ideas with your partner and agree on the best words to complete the frame.

Our teacher said we will ______________________ something new about several kinds of animals ______________________ our field trip to the zoo on Friday.

Our Turn

Discuss
Listen
Write

Read the prompt. Work with the teacher to complete the frames. Write a thoughtful response that includes a reason.

PROMPT: Imagine that you and your friends will make a fruit salad before your Fourth of July party. Explain the steps in the correct sequence.

__________________ our party, we will make a fruit salad. First, we'll wash apples and ______________________ . Next, we'll ask an adult to use a knife to __________________ the fruit. Then we'll mix it and take it to the party.

Be an Academic Author

Write
Discuss
Listen

Read the prompt and complete the frames. Strengthen your response with a reason.
PROMPT: Imagine a class field trip to a hike around a lake. Write about a problem that happened before the end of the trip.

Our field trip to the lake was almost a disaster. Our bus left the school ______________________ sunrise. We arrived at the lake at __________________ o'clock, and started on our hike. After lunch, a student fell and ____________________ her ankle, and we barely made it back to the bus by sunset.

Construct a Response

Read
Discuss
Listen

Read the prompt and write a thoughtful response. Strengthen your response with a reason.
PROMPT: Imagine that you are making a list with the names of four classmates. Describe how you would list them in alphabetical order. Why is having an alphabetical list helpful in a classroom?

____

____

____

grammar tip

A **future tense verb** tells what will happen later, or in the future. To write the future tense, add the word ***will*** before the base verb.

EXAMPLE: For my birthday party, Dad **will** make potato salad and Mom **will** grill hot dogs.

after

preposition

Say it: af • ter

 ***Write it:*** ______________ ***Write it again:*** ______________

 ______________

TOOLKIT

Meaning

coming later than something or someone else

Synonym

- later

Antonym

- before

Examples

- My dad and I always wash and dry the ______________ **after** dinner.

- Our ______________ team screamed with happiness **after** the winning goal.

Forms

Family

Word Partners

- after the/a ______ (event, e.g., party, game)
- the ______ (day/week) after ______

Examples

- Everyone in the class helped clean up the trash **after the** picnic yesterday.
- **The day after Thanksgiving** is always a holiday for students.

 **Try It**

After lunch, I usually play ______________________________ until the bell rings.

VERBAL PRACTICE

Talk about it

Discuss
Listen
Write

Discuss ideas with your partner, listen to classmates, and then write your favorite idea.

1. Our teacher let us read several ______________________________ **after** the test.

2. After the ______________________________

party, I reminded my little sister to tell our guests, "Thank you for coming!"

WRITING PRACTICE

Collaborate
Discuss
Listen
Agree
Write

Discuss ideas with your partner and agree on the best words to complete the frame.

We knew that the parents enjoyed our ____________________ because they cheered loudly ____________________ the performance.

Our Turn
Discuss
Listen
Write

Read the prompt. Work with the teacher to complete the frames. Write a thoughtful response that includes a reason.

PROMPT: Imagine that you wanted to go somewhere fun, but your parent/guardian was too busy at work to take you. Say where you went and what you did after your arrival?

Recently when my mom was at work, she gave me permission to go with my brother to the ____________________. We made sure to call her ____________________ our arrival. This helped my mother know that we were safe and ____________________.

Be an Academic Author
Write
Discuss
Listen

Read the prompt and complete the frames. Strengthen your response with an experience.

PROMPT: What does everyone in your family usually do after dinner?

____________________ dinner, the adults in my family usually watch ____________________ on TV. When I finish my homework, I usually ____________________ until I go to bed at ____________________ p.m.

Construct a Response
Read
Discuss
Listen

Read the prompt and write a thoughtful response. Strengthen your response with an experience.

PROMPT: Where do you go after school when the weather is nice? What do you do there?

____

____

____

grammar tip

A **past-tense verb** describes an action that already happened. To write the past tense, add ***-ed*** to the end of a verb.

EXAMPLE: When my cat **scratched** up the furniture, at first my dad **yelled** and then **repaired** her scratching post.

finally

adverb

Say it: fi • nal • ly

Write it: ____________ **Write it again:** ____________

 ____________

TOOLKIT

Meaning

coming after a long time or last in a series of things or actions

Synonyms

- at the end; later

Examples

- **Finally**, the ____________ is ready, so we can cook the food for the party.

- After weeks of planning, my cousins **finally** left on their vacation to ____________ .

Forms

Family

- **Adjective:** final

Word Partners

- finally (do something)
- Finally, ______

Examples

- It took a long time, but I **finally** learned how to multiply by five.
- **Finally**, after a long car chase, the police caught the thief.

 **Try It**

Our ____________ team **finally** made the winning goal at the end of the game.

VERBAL PRACTICE

Talk about it

Discuss
Listen
Write

Discuss ideas with your partner, listen to classmates, and then write your favorite idea.

1. After working hard on our kite, we **finally** got it to ____________ properly.

2. When my cousin **finally** started eating healthy foods, she felt better all the time and stopped having ____________ so often.

finally

adverb

WRITING PRACTICE

Collaborate
Discuss
Listen
Agree
Write

Discuss ideas with your partner and agree on the best words to complete the frame.

When the United States team won several games at the World Cup, soccer ______________ became a popular sport in our ______________.

Our Turn
Discuss
Listen
Write

Read the prompt. Work with the teacher to complete the frames. Write a thoughtful response that includes an experience.

PROMPT: What are you finally learning about words in the *Academic Vocabulary Toolkit?*

After studying several units, we are ______________ learning that the Toolkit words are helpful when we ______________ about any subject at school. For example, we often use the Toolkit word "______________" during ______________.

Be an Academic Author
Write
Discuss
Listen

Read the prompt and complete the frames. Strengthen your response with a reason.

PROMPT: Think about something that was difficult to learn how to do. How did you finally learn to do it?

Although it was difficult, I ______________ learned how to ______________. One thing that helped me was practicing and trying new ______________ every day.

Construct a Response
Read
Discuss
Listen

Read the prompt and write a thoughtful response. Strengthen your response with an experience.

PROMPT: Explain the steps you would follow to make a pizza with your favorite ingredients. What ingredient would you finally add to make it perfect?

____

____

____

grammar tip

An **adverb** describes an action. Adverbs usually end in ***-ly*** and come after the verb to describe how the action is done.

EXAMPLE: After the rainstorm, the earthworm **slowly** squirmed across the sidewalk.

following

adjective

Say it: fol • low • ing

Write it: ______________________ ***Write it again:*** ______________________

____

TOOLKIT

Meaning

coming at the next time, hour, day, week, month, or year

Examples

- Because it rained on Monday, there were lots of ________ to play in the **following** day.
- The ________ leaves school at the **following** times: 12 p.m. and 3 p.m.

Forms

Family

- **Verb:** follow

Word Partners

- the following (time of day: morning/afternoon/evening)
- the following (time period: hour/day/week/month/year)

Examples

- We worked in small groups to quiz each other, so we would be ready for the spelling bee **the following afternoon.**
- We plan to return from our vacation in Mexico on August 8th because the new school year starts **the following week.**

Try It

Since she no longer had symptoms of the flu, the doctor said my sister could go back to school the **following** ______________________________ .

VERBAL PRACTICE

Talk about it **Discuss ideas with your partner, listen to classmates, and then write your favorite idea.**

Discuss
Listen
Write

1. My friends and I had so much fun playing ______________________________ at recess that we decided to play again the **following** day.

2. If I want to play a game on my cousin's ______________________________ , I have to enter the **following** code: *OpenNow.*

WRITING PRACTICE

Collaborate

Discuss
Listen
Agree
Write

Discuss ideas with your partner and agree on the best words to complete the frame.

Ask the ____________ riddle: "What will you get if you cross SpongeBob with a genius?" The ____________ is "SpongeBob SmartyPants."

Our Turn

Discuss
Listen
Write

Read the prompt. Work with the teacher to complete the frames. Write a thoughtful response that includes an experience.

PROMPT: Imagine that your class went on a field trip to a farm today. What will you do at the farm? What will you do on the following day?

At the farm, each student will carefully observe one farm animal, such as (a/an) ____________ ____________. On the ____________ day we will read books and articles about the animals and write several ____________ about them.

Be an Academic Author

Write
Discuss
Listen

Read the prompt and complete the frames. Strengthen your response with a reason.

PROMPT: Explain where you might see the following sign: "Silence, please."

You might see the sign, "Silence, please," in the ____________ place: (a/an) ____________ ____________. The sign is there to remind visitors that a quiet place helps people ____________.

Construct a Response

Read
Discuss
Listen

Read the prompt and write a thoughtful response. Strengthen your response with a reason.

PROMPT: Imagine that someone gives you $1000. What will you do the following day?

____

____

____

grammar tip

A **future tense verb** tells what will happen later, or in the future. To write the future tense, add the word ***will*** before the base verb.

EXAMPLE: Before my party I **will clean** my room. Next, I **will help** Dad make cupcakes. Finally, my friends **will knock** on the door.

order

REVIEW: change *verb*

DAY 1

To make my story more interesting I decided to ______________________

the main character into a silly puppy that chases everyone out of the ☐

______________________ every morning. ☐

order *noun*

DAY 2

To wash your dog, use these steps in this ______________________:

First, pile some towels beside the bathtub. Then, ______________________ ☐

your dog in the bathtub of soapy water and get ready for your dog to splash! ☐

DAY 3

Before dinner, my father always sets the table in a special ______________________.

He puts a napkin at the left, a plate in the middle, and a ______________________ ☐

above each plate. ☐

DAY 4

In a letter to my eighty-year-old grandmother, I listed the events of this week in

______________________ by importance. The start of

______________________ vacation is the most important event, so I ☐

described it first. Then I described our new car. ☐

DAY 5

If I were a zookeeper, I would arrange the animals in ______________________

of size. I'd put big animals, such as elephants and ______________________, ☐

on one side of the zoo, and small animals on the other side. ☐

TOTAL

SMART START

REVIEW: order *noun*

DAY 1

I usually follow a certain ______________ when I pack my backpack. I put my ______________ on the bottom and my pencil case and lunch on top.

next *adjective*

DAY 2

I enjoyed the latest popular ______________ story I read, and I can't wait until ______________ year to watch the movie.

DAY 3

To be ready for the ______________ math test, our teacher reminded us to ______________ the multiplication tables the night before.

DAY 4

There are three things I always do before I go to bed. First, I put on my pajamas. The ______________ thing I do is to brush my teeth. The last thing I do is to ______________. Then I am ready for bed.

DAY 5

I like to teach my baby ______________ new words. The ______________ words I want (her/him) ______________ to learn are *nose, ears, eyes,* and *mouth*, so (she/he) ______________ can name the parts of our dog's head correctly.

TOTAL

before

REVIEW: next *adjective*

DAY 1

When you make tacos, you ______________________ the meat into a taco shell first. The ______________________ thing you do is pile on shredded cheese, lettuce, chopped tomatoes, and salsa.

before *preposition*

DAY 2

______________________ the start of a movie, we always make sure we have lots of snacks, such as ______________________, to eat as we watch the movie.

DAY 3

Our dog's hair was shaggy and matted ______________________ his bath. Now his hair is shiny and as soft as ______________________.

DAY 4

My family sits in the living room and has a brief meeting ______________________ dinner. This way we ______________________ about what happened during everyone's day.

DAY 5

Our team practiced the relay for two days ______________________ the final track meet on Friday. Our work paid off when our two best ______________________ won first and second place.

TOTAL

SMARTSTART

REVIEW: **before** ***preposition***

DAY 1

I was so hungry this morning that I ate my apple ______________________

the lunch recess. Tomorrow I will bring an extra ______________________ ☐

so I don't have this problem again. ☐

after ***preposition***

DAY 2

______________________ the movies, we always talk about the ☐

______________________ during the ride home. ☐

DAY 3

Sometimes, ______________________ an unhealthy snack, such as ☐

______________________, I get a stomach ache. ☐

DAY 4

Because it rained all day last Wednesday, we had to wear raincoats and boots

______________________ school. Even so, we were completely ☐

______________________ by the time we got home. ☐

DAY 5

______________________ my birthday, I had so many

______________________ that I didn't know what to do with them ☐

all. So I gave some to a homeless shelter. ☐

TOTAL

finally

SMART START

REVIEW: after *preposition*

DAY 1

__________ the final game, we celebrated the end of the World Cup with a big party at my __________ house.

finally *adverb*

DAY 2

__________, at the end of June, the __________ on our tree were ready to eat.

DAY 3

We discussed several ideas and __________ agreed that the best way to celebrate finishing our __________, was to have a class party.

DAY 4

By practicing for several weeks, our __________ was __________ prepared to perform for the whole school.

DAY 5

After I memorized the times table, I was __________ able to solve multiplication problems quickly and __________.

TOTAL

REVIEW: finally *adverb*

DAY 1

After watching TV for half the day on Saturday, I ______________________

decided to play ______________________ for a while.

following *adjective*

DAY 2

I stayed home from school because I had (a/an) ______________________

______________________. But the ______________________ day I

felt a lot better.

DAY 3

Name an animal with the ______________________ physical feature:

big ears. The answer is (a/an) ____________ ______________________.

DAY 4

It took longer than my parents expected to ______________________

the living room. So they decided to work on the other three rooms the

______________________ week.

DAY 5

When you have a cold, you should take the ______________________

steps: Take cough medicine; drink lots of ______________________,

and stay in bed.

TOTAL

Toolkit Unit 5 | Create

Create

Create means to make something.

To **create** a plan, solution, or an explanation, think carefully about different ways to answer a question.

To **create** stories, poems, and plays, use your imagination and explore many ideas.

 **Find It** **Read the tasks below and circle the step that would help you create a strong response.**

1. Think about the story Cinderella and write a different ending
   a. Think about what would happen if the prince never found the glass slipper.
   b. Include an elephant named Trunks.
   c. Add two more stepsisters.

2. Create a poster to convince third graders to eat more fruits and vegetables. Include two details to support your goal.
   a. Research two reasons why fruits and vegetables are important to our diet.
   b. Find out how apples and oranges grow.
   c. Learn about two new vegetables.

 **Try It** **Create a plan to convince your principal to have less homework.**

Reasons Why Students Should Get Less Homework

1. Students need time to ________________ after school.
2. Students need time to enjoy after-school activities, such as ________________.
3. Too much homework may be ________________ for some kids.

RATE WORD KNOWLEDGE

Circle the number that shows your knowledge of the words you'll use as you create pieces of writing.

RATE IT BEFORE	3rd Grade	RATE IT AFTER	4th Grade	5th Grade
1 2 3 4	**complete**	1 2 3 4	present	produce
1 2 3 4	**task**	1 2 3 4	develop	propose
1 2 3 4	**prepare**	1 2 3 4	provide	collaborate
1 2 3 4	**provide**	1 2 3 4	revise	accomplish
1 2 3 4	**organize**	1 2 3 4	demonstrate	create
1 2 3 4	**response**	1 2 3 4	elaborate	strategy

DISCUSSION GUIDE

- Form groups of four.
- Assign letters to each person.
- Each group member takes a turn leading a discussion.
- Prepare to report about one word.

A B D C

DISCUSS WORDS

Discuss how well you know the third grade words. Then, report to the class how you rated each word.

GROUP LEADER **Ask**

So, _______________ (NAME) what do you know about the word _______________?

GROUP MEMBERS **Discuss**

1 = I **have never seen or heard** the word _______________. I need to learn what it means.

2 = I **have seen or heard** the word _______________, but I need to learn the meaning.

3 = I'm **familiar** with the word _______________. I think it means _______________.

4 = I **know** the word _______________. It means _______________.

REPORTER **Report Word Knowledge**

Our group gave the word _______________ a rating of _______________.

SET A GOAL AND REFLECT

First, set a vocabulary goal for this unit by selecting at least two words that you plan to thoroughly learn. At the end of the unit, return to this page and write a reflection about one word you have mastered.

GOAL

During this unit I plan to thoroughly learn the words _______________ and _______________. Increasing my word knowledge will help me speak and write effectively when I create plans and _______________.

REFLECTION

As a result of this unit, I feel most confident about the word _______________. This is my model sentence: _______________
_______________.

complete

verb

Say it: com • **plete**

Write it: ______________ ***Write it again:*** ______________

 ______________

Meaning

to finish doing something

Synonym

- finish

Examples

- My family worked together to **complete** the 1000-piece ______________.

- When my little sister **completed** kindergarten, her ______________ had a graduation ceremony.

TOOLKIT

Forms

- **Present:**
  I/You/We/They complete
  He/She/It completes
- **Past:** completed

Family

- **Adjective:** completed

Word Partners	Examples
complete a/an/my/the *(assignment, chore)*	I have to **complete my chores** before I can play outside.
successfully complete	My brother **successfully completed** his first year of college.

 **Try It**

After I successfully **complete** my homework, I can play ______________.

VERBAL PRACTICE

Talk about it **Discuss ideas with your partner, listen to classmates, and then write your favorite idea.**

Discuss
Listen
Write

1. When my cousin **completed** his check-up at the dentist, he got to pick out (a/an) ______________ ______________.

2. I **completed** the math quiz early, so my considerate teacher asked me to ______________ quietly until everyone finished.

WRITING PRACTICE

Collaborate
Discuss
Listen
Agree
Write

Discuss ideas with your partner and agree on the best words to complete the frame.

To ________________ a game of ________________ , you must play until one person ________________________________ ________________ .

Our Turn
Discuss
Listen
Write

Read the prompt. Work with the teacher to complete the frames. Write a thoughtful response that includes a reason.
PROMPT: Think about something very difficult to complete? Why is it difficult?

I think it is very difficult to ________________ (a/an) ________________ ________________________________ . It is difficult because it takes a lot of ________________________ .

Be an Academic Author
Write
Discuss
Listen

Read the prompt and complete the frames. Strengthen your response with an experience.
PROMPT: Describe a recent school assignment that you were able to successfully complete. How did you feel once you completed it?

Recently, I worked hard to successfully ________________________ (a/an) ____________ ________________ assignment. Once I did, I felt really ________________________ .

Construct a Response
Read
Discuss
Listen

Read the prompt and write a thoughtful response. Strengthen your response with a reason.
PROMPT: Think about a chore that you have to complete every day or every week? Is it a difficult or easy chore? Why or why not?

____

____

____

grammar tip

A **present tense verb** describes an action that happens usually, sometimes, or never. If the subject of a sentence is *he, she,* or *it*, add **-s** or **-es** to the end of the verb.

EXAMPLE: During the game of tag, the person who is "it" **runs** after another person until he or she **touches**, or **tags**, the other person.

task

noun

Say it: task

Write it: ______________________ ***Write it again:*** ______________________

 ______________________

TOOLKIT

Meaning

a piece of work you have to do

Synonyms

- job, assignment

Examples

- Yesterday, I helped my father with the **task** of raking the ______________________.

- One of my favorite **tasks** is taking my dog for a ______________________.

Forms

- **Singular:** task
- **Plural:** tasks

Word Partners	Examples
• an easy/a difficult task	• My little sisters made a huge mess making pancakes, so cleaning up the kitchen was **a difficult task**.
• start/complete a task	• My brother woke up early to **complete the task** of cleaning his room.

Try It

My little cousin was given an easy **task** of picking up his ______________________ after he'd finished playing with them.

VERBAL PRACTICE

Talk about it — **Discuss ideas with your partner, listen to classmates, and then write your favorite idea.**

Discuss
Listen
Write

1. Waiters have many **tasks** to complete, like taking people's orders and bringing the ______________________.

2. Sometimes, my father will do an easy **task** like folding the laundry while he's watching ______________________ on TV.

task

noun

WRITING PRACTICE

Collaborate

Discuss
Listen
Agree
Write

Discuss ideas with your partner and agree on the best words to complete the frame.

You should not rush some ______________ like doing homework or ______________ because you might make mistakes.

Our Turn

Discuss
Listen
Write

Read the prompt. Work with the teacher to complete the frames. Write a thoughtful response that includes a reason.

PROMPT: What is one easy task that you should complete every morning? Why is it important to do this task every day?

One easy ______________ that I should complete every morning is ______________. This is an important task because it helps me have a ______________.

Be an Academic Author

Write
Discuss
Listen

Read the prompt and complete the frames. Strengthen your response with an experience.

PROMPT: Describe one difficult task that took many days to complete last summer.

Last summer, I completed a difficult ______________. It took many days for me to ______________ before the school year started.

Construct a Response

Read
Discuss
Listen

Read the prompt and write a thoughtful response. Strengthen your response with a reason.

PROMPT: Do you think children who regularly complete tasks at home should get an allowance? Why or why not?

____

____

____

grammar tip

Use the **modal verb**, or helping verb, ***should*** to suggest or recommend something. When you use ***should***, add a verb in the base form.

EXAMPLE: You **should have** lots of fruits and vegetables each day, and you **should try** to limit the amount of sugar you eat.

prepare
verb

Say it: pre • **pare**

 ***Write it:*** ____________ ***Write it again:*** ____________

 ____________

TOOLKIT

Meaning
to make someone or something ready

Synonym
- get ready

Examples
- My uncle **prepares** my cousin's ____________ before he goes to school.
- My neighbor **prepared** for his ____________ concert by practicing every day.

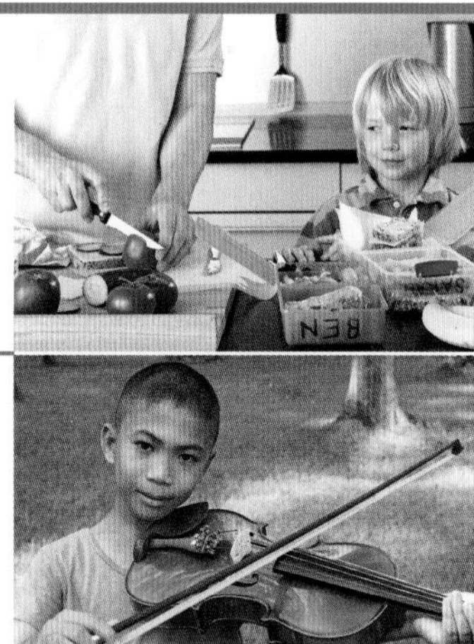

Forms
- **Present:**
  I/You/We/They prepare
  He/She/It prepares
- **Past:** prepared

Family
- **Noun:** preparation
- **Adjective:** prepared

Word Partners
- prepare ______ for ______
- prepare for ______

Examples
- Flight attendants **prepare a plane for take off** by making sure the passengers are wearing seatbelts.
- My parents **prepared for Thanksgiving** by buying a turkey.

 **Try It**
I carefully reviewed my homework to **prepare** for the ____________ test.

VERBAL PRACTICE

Talk about it — Discuss, Listen, Write

Discuss ideas with your partner, listen to classmates, and then write your favorite idea.

1. On Saturday, my uncle **prepared** lots of ____________ for the bake sale.

2. After the snowstorm, the students **prepared** to walk to school by wearing their ____________.

prepare

verb

WRITING PRACTICE

Collaborate

Discuss
Listen
Agree
Write

Discuss ideas with your partner and agree on the best words to complete the frame.

Every third grader helped ______________________________ for our class party. Some students helped by ______________________________ and others helped by decorating the classroom.

Our Turn

Discuss
Listen
Write

Read the prompt. Work with the teacher to complete the frames. Write a thoughtful response that includes a reason.

PROMPT: How can parents help prepare a young child for the first day of kindergarten?

One way that parents can help ______________________________ a child for the first day of school is by ______________________________

______________________________. This will help the child feel more

______________________________ about going to kindergarten.

Be an Academic Author

Write
Discuss
Listen

Read the prompt and complete the frames. Strengthen your response with a reason.

PROMPT: How should a family prepare for big storm?

A family should ______________ for a big storm by ______________________________

______________________________. This task is important because it helps everyone in the family feel ______________________________ during the storm.

Construct a Response

Read
Discuss
Listen

Read the prompt and write a thoughtful response. Strengthen your response with a reason.

PROMPT: What is the best way of preparing for a spelling test? Why does this task help?

____

____

____

grammar tip

Use a **verb +** ***ing*** after the prepositions ***by***, ***of***, and ***for***.

EXAMPLE: I start my day **by getting** dressed and **by eating** breakfast with my family.

provide

verb

Say it: pro • **vide**

 ***Write it:*** ______________ ***Write it again:*** ______________

 ______________

TOOLKIT

Meaning

to give something that someone needs or wants

Synonym

- give

Examples

- When my brother cut his finger at school, the __________ **provided** him with a band-aid.

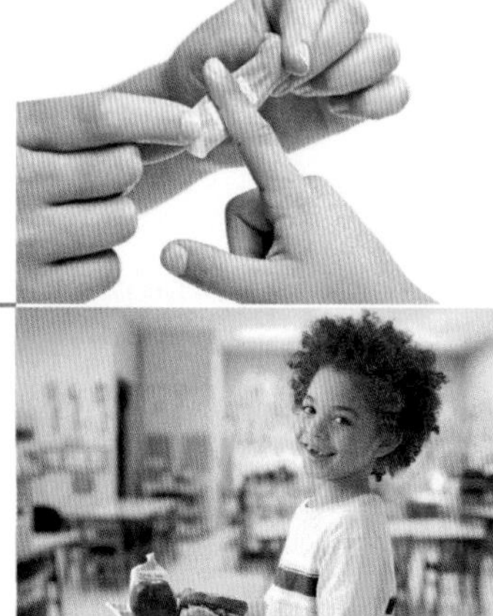

- The cafeteria **provides** two different lunch options on the __________ each day.

Forms

- **Present:**
  I/You/We/They provide
  He/She/It provides
- **Past:** provided

Word Partners

- provide (something) for (someone)
- need to provide

Examples

- The librarian **provides a list of books for the students** to read over the summer.
- I **need to provide** the title and the author's name in my book report.

 **Try It**

My mother **provided** ______________ from our garden for my aunt's party.

VERBAL PRACTICE

Talk about it **Discuss ideas with your partner, listen to classmates, and then write your favorite idea.**

Discuss
Listen
Write

1. My dad allowed us to adopt our pet from the animal shelter because we promised to **provide** a caring home for the ______________.

2. Restaurants that **provide** ______________ for children to use while waiting are my favorite.

WRITING PRACTICE

Collaborate
Discuss
Listen
Agree
Write

Discuss ideas with your partner and agree on the best words to complete the frame.

Teachers don't like to ______________ answers to students during a test, unless (a/an) ______________ ______________ is confusing to everyone.

Our Turn
Discuss
Listen
Write

Read the prompt. Work with the teacher to complete the frames. Write a thoughtful response that includes a reason.

PROMPT: What are two things that dog owners need to provide to their pets each day?

Dog owners need to ______________ their pets with plenty of ______________ each day. Without these things, a dog would become ______________.

Be an Academic Author
Write
Discuss
Listen

Read the prompt and complete the frames. Strengthen your response with a reason.

PROMPT: Do you think schools should provide one make-up day for missed homework assignments? Why or why not?

I think schools (should/should not) ______________ ______________ one make-up day for missed homework. This extra day is ______________ because it helps students learn how to ______________ assignments.

Construct a Response
Read
Discuss
Listen

Read the prompt and write a thoughtful response. Strengthen your response with a reason.

PROMPT: Do you think all schools should provide singing classes? Why or why not?

____

____

____

grammar tip

The **preposition *to*** needs to be followed by a base verb.

EXAMPLE: I wanted **to ride** my bike, but my mother said that I needed **to do** schoolwork first.

organize

verb

Say it: or • ga • nize

 ***Write it:*** ________________ ***Write it again:*** ________________

 ________________

Meaning

to put people or things into a special order; to plan an activity or event

Synonym

- arrange

Examples

- During recess the students **organized** into two ________ to play tug of war.
- My grandfather likes to **organize** the ________ in the cabinet.

TOOLKIT

Forms

- **Present:**
  I/You/We/They organize
  He/She/It organizes
- **Past:** organized

Family

- **Noun:** organization
- **Adjective:** organized

Word Partners

- organize ______ carefully/neatly/alphabetically
- organize a/an ___ *(event: party, meeting, game)*

Examples

- The librarian **organized the books alphabetically** so the students can find any books they want easily.
- My class **organized a coat drive** for the homeless shelter.

 **Try It**

The kindergartners **organized** the blocks carefully by ________________________.

VERBAL PRACTICE

Talk about it

Discuss
Listen
Write

Discuss ideas with your partner, listen to classmates, and then write your favorite idea.

1. At the start of the school year, I **organize** my ________________ carefully.

2. My sister **organized** a trip to the ________________ ________________ for our family.

organize

verb

WRITING PRACTICE

Collaborate

Discuss
Listen
Agree
Write

Discuss ideas with your partner and agree on the best words to complete the frame.

Last year, our teacher ______________________ a party to celebrate ______________________.

Our Turn

Discuss
Listen
Write

Read the prompt. Work with the teacher to complete the frames. Write a thoughtful response that includes an example.

PROMPT: Describe ways to organize a closet neatly.

The first thing to do when you ______________________ a closet neatly is to take out all of your old ______________________. Then, after trying on each pair of pants and every ______________________, carefully put everything away that still fits, and donate the rest.

Be an Academic Author

Write
Discuss
Listen

Read the prompt and complete the frames. Strengthen your response with a reason.

PROMPT: If you organized a book club, what would you want your members to read. Why?

If I ______________________ a book club, I would want the members to read ______________________ books. I would focus on these books because I think they are the most ______________________ to read.

Construct a Response

Read
Discuss
Listen

Read the prompt and write a thoughtful response. Strengthen your response with an example.

PROMPT: Think about an event that you helped organize. Describe who you helped and what you did to make it a success.

____

____

____

grammar tip

A **past-tense verb** describes an action that already happened. To make most verbs past-tense, add ***-ed*** to the ending. For verbs that end in silent *e*, simply add ***-d***.

EXAMPLE: When I **baked** the chocolate chip cookies, I **used** extra chocolate chips.

response

noun

Say it: re • **sponse**

Write it: ______________ **Write it again:** ______________

 ______________

TOOLKIT

Meaning

a spoken or written answer to a question

Synonym

- answer

Examples

- When my mother asked if I liked the __________, my **response** was "Yes!"
- After seeing his grade on the test, my friend's **response** was a big __________.

Forms

- **Singular:** response
- **Plural:** responses

Family

- **Verb:** respond

Word Partners

- a thoughtful response
- a brief/lengthy response

Examples

- It's best to give **a thoughtful response** to test questions.
- The janitor asked teachers to write **a brief response** to his survey about recycling.

 **Try It**

We shared thoughtful **responses** to solve the problem of ants in our __________.

VERBAL PRACTICE

Talk about it **Discuss ideas with your partner, listen to classmates, and then write your favorite idea.**

Discuss
Listen
Write

1. When I asked my friend to name his favorite singer, his **response** was __________.

2. I asked my brother about the __________ game, and his lengthy **response** included details about every play.

WRITING PRACTICE

Collaborate

Discuss
Listen
Agree
Write

Discuss ideas with your partner and agree on the best words to complete the frame.

Our teacher asked each of us to write a lengthy ______________________ to the principal's request for ideas about a new ______________________.

Our Turn

Discuss
Listen
Write

Read the prompt. Work with the teacher to complete the frames. Write a thoughtful response that includes a reason.

PROMPT: Which do you think are better, books or movies? Provide a brief response.

My brief ______________________ to this question is that (books/movies) ______________ are better because I think it is important to allow people to ______________________.

Be an Academic Author

Write
Discuss
Listen

Read the prompt and complete the frames. Strengthen your response with a reason.

PROMPT: If someone asked you what you wanted for your birthday, what kind of response would you provide?

I would provide a very thoughtful ______________________ to a question about what I want for my birthday. I would answer thoughtfully because then I'm more likely to receive ______________________ gifts that I would use and enjoy.

Construct a Response

Read
Discuss
Listen

Read the prompt and write a thoughtful response. Strengthen your response with a reason.

PROMPT: Do you think a third grader should be able to stay home alone for a few hours? Why or why not? Provide a thoughtful response.

____

____

____

grammar tip

The **preposition *to*** needs to be followed by a base verb.

EXAMPLE: I like **to work** in groups and **to share** ideas.

complete

REVIEW: following *adjective*

DAY 1

After spending a lot of time ______________________,

the ______________________ day my legs felt really sore.

complete *verb*

DAY 2

After my little sister ______________ her drawing, my mother

put it on the ______________________.

DAY 3

After I ______________ all the levels of the video game, I felt

______________________.

DAY 4

After I ______________ the job of washing our car, my father

gave me (a/an) ________ ______________ to say *thank you*.

DAY 5

In karate class, to move up from a white belt to a yellow belt, you need to

______________ all of the ______________ at

the white belt level.

TOTAL

SMART START

REVIEW: complete *verb*

DAY 1

After I ______________ a sculpture in art class, I gave it to my ______________ as a gift.

task *noun*

DAY 2

When my family sets the table for dinner, my parents give my five year old brother some easy ______________ like helping with the ______________.

DAY 3

Gardeners do many ______________ in a garden, such as trimming trees and ______________.

DAY 4

My parents said I could get a gerbil if I promise to do all the ______________ like cleaning its cage and ______________.

DAY 5

I don't mind doing all the ______________ that can be done outside like sweeping the sidewalk or ______________.

TOTAL

prepare

REVIEW: **task** ***noun***

DAY 1

There are some ______________________ I don't enjoy, such as cleaning my room, but there are others that I do enjoy, such as ______________________.

prepare ***verb***

DAY 2

My father always ______________________ spaghetti just the way I like it, with plenty of ______________________.

DAY 3

My teacher taught us to ______________________ for writing reports by ______________________ first.

DAY 4

Last weekend my family ______________________ for going to the beach by packing our beach bags with lots of ______________________.

DAY 5

Last year I ______________________ for Mother's Day by making my mother a ______________________.

TOTAL

SMART START

REVIEW: prepare *verb*

DAY 1

I ______________________ for the mile-run in gym class last week by

____

____.

provide *verb*

DAY 2

Every day my parents ______________________ me with a snack

such as (a/an) ____________ ______________________ when I get

home from school.

DAY 3

After the party, my friend's parents ______________________

each child with a party bag that included a ______________________.

DAY 4

Whenever we visit my aunt, she ______________________

me and my sister with lots of ______________________ to play with.

DAY 5

Earlier today our teacher ______________________ us with two choices.

We could use the extra time at the end of the day to either play a game or to

____.

TOTAL

organize

REVIEW: provide *verb*

DAY 1

Yesterday our teacher ______________________________

each student with (a/an) ______________ ______________________ ☐

before the test. ☐

organize *verb*

DAY 2

My cousin's room is so ______________________ that he can't find ☐

anything in it. He needs to ______________________ his room! ☐

DAY 3

I'm helping my parents to ______________________ my birthday

party. We're going to make crafts and ______________________ ☐

at the party. ☐

DAY 4

Last week we ______________________ all of the art room ☐

supplies by putting them into ______________________ . ☐

DAY 5

Our gym teacher often ______________________ our class into two ☐

teams to play games like basketball and ______________________ . ☐

TOTAL

REVIEW: organize *verb*

DAY 1

Right after my father neatly ______________________ all of the ______________________ on my baby sister's shelves, she pulled them all off the shelves and onto the floor! ☐ ☐

response *noun*

DAY 2

Whenever anyone asks us what we want on our pizza, our ______________________ is always "Lots of ______________________, please!" ☐ ☐

DAY 3

I felt ______________________ when my teacher asked me to share my ______________________ to the question with the class. ☐ ☐

DAY 4

When my friend asked for my opinion of the movie ______________________ ______________________, my ______________________ was that it was really entertaining. ☐ ☐

DAY 5

When my friend's mother asked her what flavor cake she wanted for her birthday, her ______________________ was that she wanted (a/an) ______________________ ______________________ cake. ☐ ☐

TOTAL

Toolkit Unit 6 | Compare and Contrast

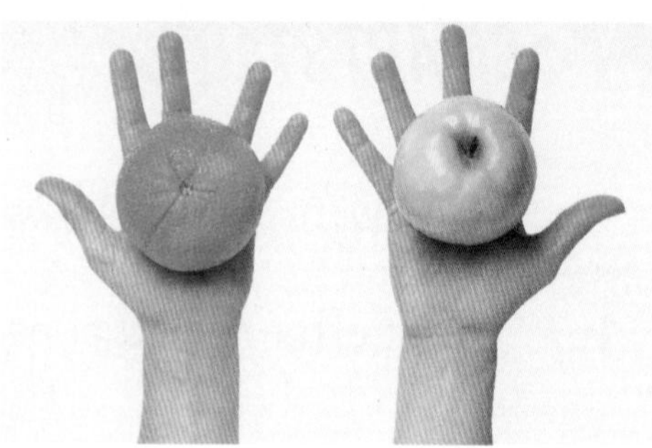

Compare and Contrast

To **compare** two or more things, analyze what is the same.

To **contrast** two or more things, analyze what is different.

 **Find It** **Compare** apples and oranges and circle what is the same.

Apples and Oranges

- are fruits
- are orange when ripe
- have sections

 **Try It** **Contrast** what is different about apples and oranges by adding ideas to each list.

Apples	**Oranges**
• the peel can be eaten	• the peel cannot be eaten
• juice has no pulp	• juice has pulp
• The peel is ____________ and smooth.	• The peel is ____________ and textured, or rough.

RATE WORD KNOWLEDGE

Circle the number that shows your knowledge of the words you'll use to compare and contrast.

RATE IT

BEFORE	3rd Grade	AFTER	4th Grade	5th Grade
1 2 3 4	**alike**	1 2 3 4	similar	comparison
1 2 3 4	**different**	1 2 3 4	difference	comparable
1 2 3 4	**similar**	1 2 3 4	similarity	contrast
1 2 3 4	**difference**	1 2 3 4	differently	identical
1 2 3 4	**similarity**	1 2 3 4	common	unique
1 2 3 4	**opposite**	1 2 3 4	unlike	differ

DISCUSSION GUIDE
- Form groups of four.
- Assign letters to each person. A B D C
- Each group member takes a turn leading a discussion.
- Prepare to report about one word.

DISCUSS WORDS

Discuss how well you know the third grade words. Then, report to the class how you rated each word.

GROUP LEADER **Ask**

So, ______ (NAME) what do you know about the word ______?

GROUP MEMBERS **Discuss**

1 = I **have never seen or heard** the word ______. I need to learn what it means.

2 = I **have seen or heard** the word ______, but I need to learn the meaning.

3 = I'm **familiar** with the word ______. I think it means ______.

4 = I **know** the word ______. It means ______.

REPORTER **Report Word Knowledge**

Our group gave the word ______ a rating of ______.

SET A GOAL AND REFLECT

First, set a vocabulary goal for this unit by selecting at least two words that you plan to thoroughly learn. At the end of the unit, return to this page and write a reflection about one word you have mastered.

GOAL

During this unit I plan to thoroughly learn the words ______ and ______. Increasing my word knowledge will help me speak and write effectively when I compare and ______.

REFLECTION

As a result of this unit, I feel most confident about the word ______. This is my model sentence: ______ ______.

alike

adjective

Say it: a • like

Write it: ______________________ ***Write it again:*** ______________________

____

TOOLKIT

Meaning

almost the same

Synonym

- similar

Antonym

- different

Examples

- Male and female birds may look **alike**, but only females lay ____________ .

- The flags of Italy and Mexico are **alike**, except that Mexico's flag has a ____________ on it.

Word Partners

- (look, act, think) alike
- exactly alike

Examples

- When my best friend and I wear the same outfit, many people say that we **look alike**.
- The twins are **exactly alike**, and sometimes I can't tell them apart.

Try It

Some real flowers and fake flowers look exactly **alike**, but the fake ones don't have a ____ scent.

VERBAL PRACTICE

Talk about it

Discuss
Listen
Write

Discuss ideas with your partner, listen to classmates, and then write your favorite idea.

1. No two ______________________________ are exactly **alike**.

2. Whole milk and lowfat milk look **alike**, but whole milk is much ______________________________ .

WRITING PRACTICE

Collaborate
Discuss
Listen
Agree
Write

Discuss ideas with your partner and agree on the best words to complete the frame.

Cell phone apps and handheld video games are ______________________

because you can play both when you are riding in a ______________________.

Our Turn
Discuss
Listen
Write

Read the prompt. Work with the teacher to complete the frames. Write a thoughtful response that includes an example.
PROMPT: Think of two holidays that are alike in some ways. How are they alike?

Two holidays that are ______________ are ______________________

and ______________________. For example, on both of these holidays,

people celebrate with ______________________________.

Be an Academic Author
Write
Discuss
Listen

Read the prompt and complete the frames. Strengthen your response with an example.
PROMPT: Think of a relative or friend who looks and acts like you. How are you alike?

My ______________________ and I look and act ______________________

in some ways. For example, I have ______________________ and (he/she)

______________ does too. Also, we both enjoy playing ______________________

on the weekend.

Construct a Response
Write
Discuss
Listen

Read the prompt and write a thoughtful response. Strengthen your response with an example.
PROMPT: Think of two sports that are alike in some way. How are they alike?

____

____

____

grammar tip

Count nouns name things that can be counted. Count nouns have two forms, singular and plural. To make most count nouns plural, add **-s**.

EXAMPLE: Our **neighbors** have two **horses.**

different

adjective

Say it: dif • fer • ent

Write it: ____________________ **Write it again:** ____________________

 ____________________

TOOLKIT

Meaning

not the same as something or someone else

Synonym

- not alike

Antonym

- alike

Examples

- In the past, ____________ looked **different** from the way they look today.

- Frogs and toads have **different** ____________.

Family

- **Noun:** difference
- **Adverb:** differently

Word Partners

- be different from
- (look, seem, feel, sound, taste) different

Examples

- Dolphins **are different from** sharks in an important way. Dolphins are mammals, and sharks are fish.
- The teacher cut her hair short, and now she **looks different**.

 **Try It**

Riding on a bus **is different from** riding in a car. Cars are ____________________.

VERBAL PRACTICE

Talk about it
Discuss
Listen
Write

Discuss ideas with your partner, listen to classmates, and then write your favorite idea.

1. Solitary sports, like running, are very **different** from team sports, like ____________________.

2. Sometimes I eat cereal in the morning, but I really prefer something that tastes **different**, such as ____________________.

different

adjective

WRITING PRACTICE

Collaborate
Discuss
Listen
Agree
Write

Discuss ideas with your partner and agree on the best words to complete the frame.

Third grade is ______________________ from second grade because now we ______________________.

Our Turn
Discuss
Listen
Write

Read the prompt. Work with the teacher to complete the frames. Write a thoughtful response that includes a reason.

PROMPT: Think of two different desserts that you enjoy. How are they different?

Two desserts that I enjoy are ______________________ and ______________________. These desserts taste ______________________ because one is ______________________ and the other is ______________________.

Be an Academic Author
Write
Discuss
Listen

Read the prompt and complete the frames. Strengthen your response with an example.

PROMPT: What is one way that your best friend and you are different?

My best friend and I are ______________________ in one way. For example, I am ______________________, but my best friend is ______________________.

Construct a Response
Write
Discuss
Listen

Read the prompt and write a thoughtful response. Strengthen your response with a reason.

PROMPT: Think about an activity that you do often during the summer and one you do in winter. How is one activity different from the other?

____

____

____

grammar tip

An **adjective** describes, or tells about, a noun. An adjective sometimes appears after verbs such as *is, are, look, feel, smell,* and *taste.*

EXAMPLE: Roses are **beautiful**, and they smell **sweet**.

similar

adjective

Say it: sim • i • lar

Write it: ____________________ ***Write it again:*** ____________________

 ____________________

TOOLKIT

Meaning

almost the same, but not exactly

Synonym

- alike

Antonym

- different

Examples

- Tigers and leopards look **similar**, but leopards have ____________ on their fur.

- A red light and a ____________ sign have **similar** meanings.

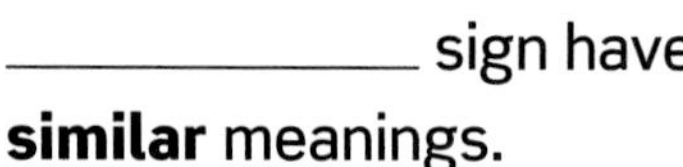

Family

- **Noun:** similarity
- **Adverb:** similarly

Word Partners

- be similar to someone/something
- (feel, look, sound, taste) similar

Examples

- *Twinkle, Twinkle Little Star* **is similar to** the *ABC Song* because they have the same tune.
- Cranberry juice **looks similar** to fruit punch, but they have different tastes.

 **Try It**

Many backpacks look **similar**, but mine has different ______________________________ .

VERBAL PRACTICE

Talk about it

Discuss
Listen
Write

Discuss ideas with your partner, listen to classmates, and then write your favorite idea.

1. My handwriting looks **similar** to my sister's handwriting, but mine is

____ .

2. I saw a ______________________ I liked in an expensive clothing store, but then I found a **similar** one in the next store that was on sale.

WRITING PRACTICE

Collaborate
Discuss
Listen
Agree
Write

Discuss ideas with your partner and agree on the best words to complete the frame.

Synonyms are words that have ______________________ meanings. For example, a synonym for *difficult* is ______________________.

Our Turn
Discuss
Listen
Write

Read the prompt. Work with the teacher to complete the frames. Write a thoughtful response that includes an example.
PROMPT: Describe a movie or program that you and a friend have similar ideas about.

My friend and I have ______________________ ideas about the movie ______________________. For example, we both think it is clever and ______________________.

Be an Academic Author
Write
Discuss
Listen

Read the prompt and complete the frames. Strengthen your response with a reason.
PROMPT: Think about two similar things you like to eat for lunch. How are they similar foods?

Two of my favorite things to eat for lunch are ______________________ and ______________________. These are ______________________ foods because they both taste ______________________.

Construct a Response
Write
Discuss
Listen

Read the prompt and write a thoughtful response. Strengthen your response with an example.
PROMPT: Think of two characters you've read about who are similar in some way. How is one character similar to the other?

____

____

____

grammar tip

Adjectives are always singular even if they describe a plural noun. Do not add **-s** to adjectives that describe plural nouns.

EXAMPLE: Lorde and Taylor Swift are **talented** singers.

difference

noun

Say it: dif • fer • ence

Write it: ______________ **Write it again:** ______________

 ______________

TOOLKIT

Meaning

the way one thing is not the same as something else

Antonym

- similarity

Examples

- The twins look the same, except for the **difference** in the length of their ______________.

- One **difference** between apes and monkeys is that only monkeys have ______________.

Forms

- **Singular:** difference
- **Plural:** differences

Family

- **Adjective:** different
- **Adverb:** differently

Word Partners

- the difference between ______ and ______
- main/important difference

Examples

- **The difference between** fiction and nonfiction is that fictional stories aren't real, and nonfiction stories are true.
- The **main difference** between fruits and vegetables is that fruits have seeds and vegetables don't.

 **Try It**

The **difference** between cars and trucks is that trucks are ______________.

VERBAL PRACTICE

Talk about it

Discuss
Listen
Write

Discuss ideas with your partner, listen to classmates, and then write your favorite idea.

1. Team players wear similar uniforms, but there are often **differences** in their ______________.

2. To teach the **difference** between *quiet* and *loud*, the kindergarten teacher whispered and then ______________.

difference

noun

WRITING PRACTICE

Collaborate
Discuss
Listen
Agree
Write

Discuss ideas with your partner and agree on the best words to complete the frame.

An important _______________ between picture books and chapter books is that chapter books are _______________.

Our Turn
Discuss
Listen
Write

Read the prompt. Work with the teacher to complete the frames. Write a thoughtful response that includes an example.

PROMPT: What is the difference between preschool and third grade?

The _______________ between preschool and third grade is that what we're learning is more _______________. For example, we are learning about _______________, while preschoolers do activities like coloring and learning the alphabet.

Be an Academic Author
Write
Discuss
Listen

Read the prompt and complete the frames. Strengthen your response with an example.

PROMPT: Think of a kind of food from another culture, such as Italian, Indian, or Vietnamese food. What is the difference between this food and American food?

The main _______________ between _______________ foods and American foods is that many dishes from that culture are _______________. For example, _______________ tastes nothing like an American hot dog.

Construct a Response
Write
Discuss
Listen

Read the prompt and write a thoughtful response. Strengthen your response with an example.

PROMPT: Describe one important difference between a real friend and someone who is not.

____

____

____

grammar tip

An **adjective** describes, or tells about, a noun. Usually an adjective goes before the noun it describes.

EXAMPLE: The **delicate** egg fell on the **hard** floor.

similarity

noun

Say it: sim • i • **lar** • i • ty

 **Write it:** ____________ **Write it again:** ____________

____

TOOLKIT

Meaning

something that is the same about two things or people

Antonym

- difference

Examples

- One **similarity** between the boy's ____________ and his father's is their smile.

- There are many **similarities** between horses and zebras, but only zebras have ____________ .

Forms

- **Singular:** similarity
- **Plural:** similarities

Family

- **Adjective:** similar
- **Adverb:** similarly

Word Partners

- (few, some, many) similarities between ______ and ______
- strong similarity

Examples

- There are **many similarities between cucumbers and zucchini.**
- There is a **strong similarity** in the words for "mama" in many languages, such as *mama* in Arabic, and *ma* in Hindi.

 **Try It**

There is often a strong **similarity** between children and their ____________ .

VERBAL PRACTICE

Talk about it

Discuss
Listen
Write

Discuss ideas with your partner, listen to classmates, and then write your favorite idea.

1. There are few **similarities** between the clothes my ____________ and I wear.

2. The strong **similarity** between oranges and grapefruits is that they are both ____________ .

similarity

noun

WRITING PRACTICE

Collaborate

Discuss
Listen
Agree
Write

Discuss ideas with your partner and agree on the best words to complete the frame.

There are many ______________ between the symptoms of a cold and an allergy, because both can make a person ______________.

Our Turn

Discuss
Listen
Write

Read the prompt. Work with the teacher to complete the frames. Write a thoughtful response that includes an experience.

PROMPT: Think of two teachers you know. What is a strong similarity between them?

There is a strong ______________ between ______________ and ______________. In my experience, both of these teachers are really ______________.

Be an Academic Author

Write
Discuss
Listen

Read the prompt and complete the frames. Strengthen your response with an example.

PROMPT: Think of two TV programs you watch. What is a strong similarity between them?

Two TV programs I watch are ______________ and ______________. A strong ______________ between them is that they are both very ______________.

Construct a Response

Read
Discuss
Listen

Read the prompt and write a thoughtful response. Strengthen your response with an example.

PROMPT: Think of two animals. Describe several similarities between the two animals.

____

____

____

grammar tip

Quantity adjectives tell "how much" or "how many." Quantity adjectives go before a plural noun. Common quantity adjectives are: *most, many, some, several, both.*

EXAMPLE: Many students check out **several** library books each week.

opposite

adjective

Say it: **op** • po • site

Write it: ______________ ***Write it again:*** ______________

 ______________

TOOLKIT

Meaning

totally different

Synonym

- different

Examples

- Happiness and ____________ are **opposite** feelings.

- I'm very messy, but my sister has the **opposite** personality.

  She's very ____________ .

Family

- **Verb:** oppose

Word Partners

- have opposite (looks, tastes, ideas)
- the exact opposite

Examples

- I enjoy action movies, but my sisters **have opposite tastes** because they prefer movies about love.
- My short, curly hair is **the exact opposite** style from my brother's short, straight hair.

 **Try It**

Boots and ______________________ are **opposite** shoe styles.

VERBAL PRACTICE

Talk about it Discuss ideas with your partner, listen to classmates, and then write your favorite idea.

Discuss
Listen
Write

1. A crow and (a/an) ____________ ______________________ are the exact **opposite** color.

2. Many older cats are lazy, but kittens have **opposite** personalities because they love to ______________________ .

opposite

adjective

WRITING PRACTICE

Collaborate
Discuss
Listen
Agree
Write

Discuss ideas with your partner and agree on the best words to complete the frame.

A word that has the exact ______________________ meaning of the word *tiny* is ______________________.

Our Turn
Discuss
Listen
Write

Read the prompt. Work with the teacher to complete the frames. Write a thoughtful response that includes an example.

PROMPT: What activity do you and your friend have opposite ideas about?

My friend and I have ______________________ ideas about ______________________. For example, my friend thinks it is ______________________, but I disagree.

Be an Academic Author
Write
Discuss
Listen

Read the prompt and complete the frames. Strengthen your response with an experience.

PROMPT: Describe a time when you started a book and felt one way, but at the end you had the opposite feeling.

Once, when I started reading ______________________, I thought it seemed ______________________. By the time I finished it, I had the ______________________ feeling: I thought it was really ______________________!

Construct a Response
Read
Discuss
Listen

Read the prompt and write a thoughtful response. Strengthen your response with an example.

PROMPT: What is something that you and your parents have opposite ideas about?

____

____

____

grammar tip

An **adjective** describes, or tells about, a noun. Usually an adjective goes before the noun it describes.

EXAMPLE: The **new** student asked an **interesting** question.

alike

SMART START

REVIEW: response *noun*

DAY 1

When my friend asked me to name my favorite movie, my ________________

was ____.

alike *adjective*

DAY 2

My best friend and I are so ________________ that we often have

the exact same ________________ even when we are not together.

DAY 3

Sugar and salt look exactly ________________, so be careful not

to put salt in your ________________________ by mistake!

DAY 4

The expensive brand of ________________ and the cheaper brand

are so ________________________, we can't tell them apart.

DAY 5

Twins may look ________________________, but their

________________________ may not be the same at all.

TOTAL

SMART START

REVIEW: alike *adjective*

DAY 1

My backpack and lunch box look ________________ because they both have the same ________________.

different *adjective*

DAY 2

At first I liked the rice, but then my father added ________________, and now it tastes ________________.

DAY 3

Good friends can have very ________________ ideas about things like ________________, but they can still get along well.

DAY 4

The clothes I wear now are ________________ from the clothes I wore a few years ago. Now, I never wear ________________.

DAY 5

Homemade desserts taste ________________ from store-bought treats. I love to eat homemade ________________.

TOTAL

similar

SMART START

REVIEW: different *adjective*

DAY 1

Cats and dogs often have ______________________ personalities. Dogs are often friendly and playful while some cats can be ______________________ .

similar *adjective*

DAY 2

Newspapers and magazines are ______________________ to each other in certain ways. For example, they both include ______________________ .

DAY 3

Some fairy tales seem ______________________ because they have the same kinds of characters. For example, many fairy tales include characters like ______________________ .

DAY 4

Ice cream flavors such as chocolate and ______________________ have ______________________ tastes.

DAY 5

A security guard's job is ______________________ to a police officer's job. Both have to keep people or things ______________________ .

TOTAL

REVIEW: similar *adjective*

DAY 1

The words *can* and *man* sound ________________, as do the words *cat* and ________________.

difference *noun*

DAY 2

The mother helped the toddler understand the ________________ between *big* and *small* by pointing to pictures of an elephant for *big* and (a/an) ________ ________________ for small.

DAY 3

Sweeping and vacuuming both clean the floor, but the ________________ is that vacuuming is ________________.

DAY 4

Two important ________________ between healthy snacks, like apples, and treats like ________________ is to enjoy the healthy foods more often and eat the treats once in awhile.

DAY 5

My friend and I have similar notebooks. The main ________________ between them is that I have ________________ on mine and (he/she) ________________ doesn't.

TOTAL

similarity

REVIEW: difference *noun*

DAY 1

To show a toddler the ______________________

between the words *open* and *close*, say the words while you open and close a

______________________ a few times.

similarity *noun*

DAY 2

There are some ______________________ between my

cousin's town and mine. They both have a park and (a/an) ______________________

______________________.

DAY 3

There are many ______________________ between Superman

and Spider-man. For example, they both ______________________.

DAY 4

One ______________________ between brownies and chocolate

cookies is that they are both ______________________.

DAY 5

A ______________________ between bees and wasps is that they

both can ______________________.

TOTAL

REVIEW: similarity *noun*

DAY 1

There are some ______________________ between witches and wizards in storybooks. They are both ______________________ characters.

opposite *adjective*

DAY 2

A word that has the ______________________ meaning of *slow* is ______________________.

DAY 3

My neighbor is outgoing and confident, but his younger brother has the exact ______________________ personality. The younger brother is ______________________.

DAY 4

My classmate said that the test would be easy, but we thought it was the ______________________. It was actually really ______________________.

DAY 5

After the vet gave my pet a shot to calm him down, my dog had the exact ______________________ reaction, and he started ______________________ for hours.

TOTAL

Toolkit Unit 7 | Inference

Inference

To make an **inference**, use a picture or information from text and what we already know to form an idea.

 **Find It** Look at the picture above. Answer each question and make an **inference**.

What do you already know?	+	What do you see in the picture?	=	My inference
I already know that puddles form after it rains.		I see someone in rain boots jumping in a ________ .		I think that it must have ________ earlier in the day.

 **Try It** Look at the picture. Answer each question and make an **inference**.

EMERGENCY →

What do you already know?	+	What do you see?	=	My inference
I already know that people go to the hospital when they have an emergency.		I see a picture of a sign with the word ________ on it.		I think that this picture was probably taken at a ________ .

RATE WORD KNOWLEDGE

Rate how well you know Toolkit words you'll use when you prepare to argue.

RATE IT				
BEFORE	3rd Grade	AFTER	4th Grade	5th Grade
1 2 3 4	**decide**	1 2 3 4	conclude	interpret
1 2 3 4	**predict**	1 2 3 4	assume	infer
1 2 3 4	**figure out**	1 2 3 4	conclusion	deduce
1 2 3 4	**probably**	1 2 3 4	assumption	context
1 2 3 4	**clue**	1 2 3 4	determine	presume
1 2 3 4	**prediction**	1 2 3 4	communicate	imply

DISCUSSION GUIDE

- Form groups of four.
- Assign letters to each person.
- Each group member takes a turn leading a discussion.
- Prepare to report about one word.

DISCUSS WORDS

Discuss how well you know the third grade words. Then, report to the class how you rated each word.

GROUP LEADER **Ask**

So, ______ (NAME) what do you know about the word ______ ?

GROUP MEMBERS **Discuss**

1 = I **have never seen or heard** the word ______ . I need to learn what it means.

2 = I **have seen or heard** the word ______ , but I need to learn the meaning.

3 = I'm **familiar** with the word ______ . I think it means ______ .

4 = I **know** the word ______ . It means ______ .

REPORTER **Report Word Knowledge**

Our group gave the word ______ a rating of ______ .

SET A GOAL AND REFLECT

First, set a vocabulary goal for this unit by selecting at least two words that you plan to thoroughly learn. At the end of the unit, return to this page and write a reflection about one word you have mastered.

GOAL

During this unit I plan to thoroughly learn the words ______ and ______ . Increasing my word knowledge will help me speak and write effectively when I make an ______ .

REFLECTION

As a result of this unit, I feel most confident about the word ______ . This is my model sentence: ______ ______ .

decide

verb

Say it: de • cide

Write it: ______________________ ***Write it again:*** ______________________

____

TOOLKIT

Meaning

to choose what you are going to do after thinking about it carefully

Synonym

- choose

Examples

- It is hard to **decide** which kind of ____________ to eat because they all look delicious.

- My sister **decided** to take a ____________ class after seeing a movie about it.

Forms

- **Present**
  I/You/We/They decide
  He/She/It decides
- **Past** decided

Family

- **Noun:** decision

Word Partners

- decide to (verb) instead of (verb + ing)
- decide that

Examples

- My teacher **decided to** change the seating chart each month **instead of** keeping us at the same desk all year.
- When you see how fascinating aquariums are, you might **decide that** you really want one!

Try It

My mother **decided** to allow me to ______________________________________.

VERBAL PRACTICE

Talk about it

Discuss
Listen
Write

Discuss ideas with your partner, listen to classmates, and then write your favorite idea.

1. After talking about which game to play at recess, my friends and I **decided** to play ______________________________________.

2. During soccer practice our coach had a bad ____________________, so he **decided** to end the drills early.

WRITING PRACTICE

Collaborate
Discuss
Listen
Agree
Write

Discuss ideas with your partner and agree on the best words to complete the frame.

Our teacher ____________ that if we did a good job on our reports she'd let us ____________.

Our Turn
Discuss
Listen
Write

Read the prompt. Work with the teacher to complete the frames. Write a response that includes an experience.

PROMPT: For your last birthday, what did you decide that you wanted to do? Was it a success?

For my last birthday, I ____________ that I wanted to ____________. It (was/wasn't) ____________ a success because it was a very ____________ day!

Be an Academic Author
Write
Discuss
Listen

Read the prompt and complete the frames. Strengthen your response with a reason.

PROMPT: If you and your classmates could choose one classroom activity, what would you decide to do and why?

If my classmates and I could choose a classroom activity, we would ____________ to ____________. This would be fun because it's (a/an) ____________ ____________ way to practice what we learned.

Construct a Response
Read
Discuss
Listen

Read the prompt and write a thoughtful response. Strengthen your response with an experience.

PROMPT: Think of a time you had to decide what to wear during the winter. What did you decide to wear and what happened?

____

____

____

grammar tip

A **past-tense verb** describes an action that already happened. For verbs that end in silent **e**, drop the final **e** before you add ***-ed***.

EXAMPLE: I **decorated** my notebook with stickers, but then I **changed** my mind and **removed** them.

predict

verb

Say it: pre • dict

 **Write it:** ____________________ **Write it again:** ____________________

 ____________________

TOOLKIT

Meaning

to say that something will happen in the future

Synonym

- guess

Examples

- When I see dark clouds in the sky, I often **predict** that it will ____________.

- The audience **predicted** that a rabbit would come out of the magician's ____________.

Forms

- **Present:**
  I/You/We/They predict
  He/She/It predicts
- **Past:** predicted

Family

- **Noun:** prediction

Word Partners

- predict that (something will happen)
- predict the results of

Examples

- My sister studied for the spelling test for hours, so I **predict that she will** get an A.
- The students running for class president are all well liked so we can't **predict the results of** the election.

 **Try It**

We **predicted** the results of the ____________________ contest correctly.

VERBAL PRACTICE

Talk about it **Discuss ideas with your partner, listen to classmates, and then write your favorite idea.**

Discuss
Listen
Write

1. On the first day of school our principal **predicted** that it would be a ____________________ school year.

2. In a book I read, I correctly **predicted** that the main character would become (a/an) ____________ ____________________.

predict

verb

WRITING PRACTICE

Collaborate
Discuss
Listen
Agree
Write

Discuss ideas with your partner and agree on the best words to complete the frame.

We ________________ that at the end of the school year our class will

____.

Our Turn
Discuss
Listen
Write

Read the prompt. Work with the teacher to complete the frames. Write a thoughtful response that includes a reason.

PROMPT: What grades do you predict you will receive on your report card this year? Why?

This year, I ____________ that I will receive ________________ grades on my report card because I am ________________ in class.

Be an Academic Author
Write
Discuss
Listen

Read the prompt and complete the frames. Strengthen your response with a reason.

PROMPT: What job do you predict you will have when you are an adult and why?

I ________________ that I will have a job as (a/an) ________________

________________ when I'm an adult because I enjoy

____.

Construct a Response
Read
Discuss
Listen

Read the prompt and write a thoughtful response. Strengthen your response with a reason.

PROMPT: How do you predict elementary school will be different in 100 years?

____

____

____

____

grammar tip

A **future tense verb** tells what will happen later, or in the future. To write the future tense, add the word *will* before the base verb.

EXAMPLE: Next week my class **will** go on a field trip to a real dairy farm. I think it **will** be fun!

figure out

verb

Say it: fig • ure out

 ***Write it:*** ______________ ***Write it again:*** ______________

 ______________

TOOLKIT

Meaning

to find a way to do something or to understand something difficult

Examples

- My grandfather likes to **figure out** crossword __________ .

- I tried to **figure out** how to use my mother's __________ cell phone.

Forms

- **Present:**
  I/You/We/They figure out
  He/She/It figures out
- **Past:** figured out

Word Partners

- figure out how to do something
- figure out the answer

Examples

- I **figured out how to fix** my bike by watching a video.
- Before I ask for help with a math problem, I try to **figure out the answer** on my own.

 **Try It**

Before taking gymnastics, my friend couldn't **figure out** how to do a ______________ .

VERBAL PRACTICE

Talk about it **Discuss ideas with your partner, listen to classmates, and then write your favorite idea.**

Discuss
Listen
Write

1. It took a while, but my family and I finally **figured out** that (a/an) ______________ ______________ was making the odd noises we heard outside.

2. Last week my baby cousin **figured out** how to turn on the ______________ and now she won't leave it alone!

figure out

verb

WRITING PRACTICE

Collaborate
Discuss
Listen
Agree
Write

Discuss ideas with your partner and agree on the best words to complete the frame.

Earlier this year, our class ______________________________

how to ______________________________.

Our Turn
Discuss
Listen
Write

Read the prompt. Work with the teacher to complete the frames. Write a thoughtful response that includes an experience.

PROMPT: Think of something you figured out how to do in kindergarten. How did you feel?

I ____________________ how to ______________________________

when I was in kindergarten. This made me feel ____________________.

Be an Academic Author
Write
Discuss
Listen

Read the prompt and complete the frames. Strengthen your response with an experience.

PROMPT: What was something difficult for you to figure out how to do? Who helped you?

It was difficult for me to ______________________________ how to

____________________. My ______________________________

helped me learn to do this.

Construct a Response
Read
Discuss
Listen

Read the prompt and write a thoughtful response. Strengthen your response with an experience.

PROMPT: Think of a gift you gave someone. How did you figure out what to give the person?

____

____

____

grammar tip

A **past-tense verb** describes an action that already happened. For verbs that end in silent **e**, drop the final **e** before you add ***-ed***.

EXAMPLE: My new friend invit**ed** me to her party.

probably

adverb

Say it: prob • a • bly

Write it: ______________ **Write it again:** ______________

 ______________

TOOLKIT

Meaning

likely to happen or be true

Synonym

- likely

Examples

- My classmate fixed her broken ______________ with tape, but she'll **probably** need new ones.

- My friend needs a ______________ to wear to her cousin's wedding and will **probably** buy the blue one.

Family

- **Adjective:** probable

Word Partners

- will probably (do something)
- will probably be (difficult, late)

Examples

- My partner didn't finish her assignment in class, so she **will probably** have to complete it during recess.
- It **will probably be** hot at the park, so we should bring water.

 **Try It**

I will **probably** dress as (a/an) ______________ ______________ for Halloween.

VERBAL PRACTICE

Talk about it **Discuss ideas with your partner, listen to classmates, and then write your favorite idea.**

Discuss
Listen
Write

1. I'm very exhausted so I think I will **probably** just stay home and ______________ this afternoon.

2. If you go on a nature hike, you should bring (a/an) ______________ ______________ with you because you'll **probably** get hungry.

probably

adverb

WRITING PRACTICE

Collaborate

Discuss
Listen
Agree
Write

Discuss ideas with your partner and agree on the best words to complete the frame.

We will ____________ work on ____________________ in class this week.

Our Turn

Discuss
Listen
Write

Read the prompt. Work with the teacher to complete the frames. Write a response that includes a reason.

PROMPT: What will you probably do when you get home from school today? Why?

When I get home from school, today I will ____________________

unpack my backpack and then ____________________

because I feel ____________________.

Be an Academic Author

Write
Discuss
Listen

Read the prompt and complete the frames. Strengthen your response with a reason.

PROMPT: What will you probably do this summer?

This summer I will ____________ have a lot of fun because I plan to

____________________ with my friends. This is a great activity that

we try to do every ____________________ during the summer.

Construct a Response

Read
Discuss
Listen

Read the prompt and conduct a thoughtful response. Include a reason.

PROMPT: When you are an adult, will you probably live in the same town or city you live in now? Why or why not?

____

____

____

grammar tip

An **adverb** describes an action. Adverbs usually end in ***-ly*** and come after the verb to describe how the action is done.

EXAMPLE: My little sister skated **slowly** and **carefully** across the ice.

clue

noun

Say it: clue

 ***Write it:*** ______________ ***Write it again:*** ______________

 ______________

TOOLKIT

Meaning

a piece of information that helps you find the right answer or understand something difficult

Synonym

- hint

Examples

- The man looked for **clues** to figure out who owned the lost __________.

- My aunt gave me two **clues**, but I still couldn't guess what was inside the __________.

Forms

- **Singular:** clue
- **Plural:** clues

Word Partners	Examples
• look for/search for clues	• The firefighters **looked for clues** to help them figure out what started the fire.
• a valuable/important clue	• Tests give a doctor **valuable clues** about why a patient doesn't feel well.

 **Try It**

When my dog started ______________________, it gave us a **clue** that someone was coming to the door.

VERBAL PRACTICE

Talk about it **Discuss ideas with your partner, listen to classmates, and then write your favorite idea.**

Discuss
Listen
Write

1. My first **clue** that my grandfather had come to visit was the scent of his ______________________.

2. When a baby cries, it can be an important **clue** that he or she is ______________________.

clue

noun

WRITING PRACTICE

Collaborate
Discuss
Listen
Agree
Write

Discuss ideas with your partner and agree on the best words to complete the frame.

The huge smile on our teacher's face might be a ______________ that we did a good job on our ______________ reports.

Our Turn
Discuss
Listen
Write

Read the prompt. Work with the teacher to complete the frames. Write a thoughtful response that includes an example.

PROMPT: Before you start a book, what clues might help you decide if it will be a good story to read?

Before I start book, I look for ______________ about how ______________ the story might be when I read it. For example, I look at the ______________ for clues about the story.

Be an Academic Author
Write
Discuss
Listen

Read the prompt and complete the frames. Strengthen your response with an example.

PROMPT: What valuable clues might tell you that you are near home after a long car ride?

After a long car ride, I look for valuable ______________ that might tell me I am near my home. For example, seeing some familiar ______________ usually means I'm almost home.

Construct a Response
Write
Discuss
Listen

Read the prompt and write a thoughtful response. Strengthen your response with an example.

PROMPT: Imagine your family is at a pet shelter to adopt a cat. What clues might tell you that a cat is friendly?

____

____

____

grammar tip

Use the **modal verb**, or helping verb, *might* to show that something is possible. When you use *might*, add a verb in the base form.

EXAMPLE: Our music teacher **might** let us take our recorders home during the holiday break.

prediction

noun

Say it: pre • **dic** • tion

Write it: ____________________ ***Write it again:*** ____________________

____

TOOLKIT

Meaning

something that you say will happen in the future

Synonym

- a guess

Examples

- My **prediction** is that my aunt's ____________ is a boy. 
- The group's **prediction** was that their ____________ would erupt when they added vinegar to the baking soda.

Forms

- **Singular:** prediction
- **Plural:** predictions

Family

- **Verb:** predict

Word Partners	Examples
• make a prediction about	• Sometimes when we're reading a story, we stop and **make a prediction about** what we think is going to happen next.
• correct/incorrect prediction	• The preschooler made a **correct prediction** that mixing yellow and blue paint makes the paint turn green.

Try It

Looking at the ____________________ in a book can help you make **predictions** about the story.

VERBAL PRACTICE

Talk about it — Discuss, Listen, Write

Discuss ideas with your partner, listen to classmates, and then write your favorite idea.

1. The weather reporter made a correct **prediction** when she said it was going to be ______________________________ today!
2. My **prediction** is that if you leave popsicles and ____________________ on the counter on a warm day, they will melt.

prediction

noun

WRITING PRACTICE

Collaborate

Discuss
Listen
Agree
Write

Discuss ideas with your partner and agree on the best words to complete the frame.

Our ______________________ is that ______________________

is going to become even more popular with music fans next year.

Our Turn

Discuss
Listen
Write

Read the prompt. Work with the teacher to complete the frames. Write a thoughtful response that includes an example.

PROMPT: Make a prediction about how people are going to travel in the future.

My ______________________ is that people are going to travel to other

countries or planets in new ways in the future. For example, I think people will travel

(in/on) ____________ ______________________

to go to ______________________.

Be an Academic Author

Write
Discuss
Listen

Read the prompt and complete the frames. Strengthen your response with an experience.

PROMPT: Think of a book you recently read and a prediction you made about the ending. Was your prediction correct?

I recently read ______________________. Before I finished, I made a

______________________ that it would have a ______________________

ending. I turned out to be (right/wrong) ______________________.

Construct a Response

Read
Discuss
Listen

Read the prompt and write a thoughtful response. Strengthen your response with an experience.

PROMPT: Describe an incorrect prediction you once made about a chore.

____

____

____

grammar tip

A **future tense verb** tells what will happen later, or in the future. To write the future tense, add the phrase *am going to, is going to,* or *are going to* before the base verb.

EXAMPLE: In the future, I think people **are going to** live to be 200!

decide

SMART START

REVIEW: opposite *adjective*

DAY 1

On the ______________________ side of the street from where I live, ☐

there is (a/an) ______________ ______________________. ☐

decide *verb*

DAY 2

At the supermarket, my mother usually ______________________ ☐

to buy whichever brand of ______________________ is on sale. ☐

DAY 3

My dog refused to get up this afternoon. He ______________ that he was ☐

more interested in sleeping than in ______________________ with me. ☐

DAY 4

A few weeks ago, my parents ______________________ ☐

that I need to start helping to ______________________. ☐

DAY 5

After seeing my friend eating a ______________________ ☐

at the picnic, I ______________________ to get one too. ☐

TOTAL

REVIEW: decide *verb*

DAY 1

After thinking about it for a while, I finally ____________

to buy a ____________

with the money I got for my birthday.

predict *verb*

DAY 2

One student won't stop talking in class. I ____________

that if he doesn't stop soon, the annoyed substitute teacher will

____________.

DAY 3

I have talked so much about wanting a ____________

that I ____________ my parents will get me one for my birthday.

DAY 4

If the little boy keeps spinning in circles, I ____________

he's going to ____________.

DAY 5

My family is going on a long car ride this weekend. I ____________

that my brother and I will ____________ in the car.

TOTAL

figure out

SMART*START*

REVIEW: predict *verb*

DAY 1

If you keep jumping on the bed, I ______________________

you'll ______________________ .

figure out *verb*

DAY 2

When I first ______________ how to sound out words, I felt

very ______________________ .

DAY 3

My neighbor's dog recently ______________ how to

______________________ , and now he does it

all the time.

DAY 4

If you read the directions carefully, you can ______________

how to put together a model ______________________ .

DAY 5

The first time I played the video game ______________________ ,

I didn't understand it, but with practice I ______________

how to play it.

TOTAL

REVIEW: figure out *verb*

DAY 1

It took me a long time to ______________________ how to unlock the ______________________, but I finally did!

probably *adverb*

DAY 2

My little brother will ______________________ eat all of the rice on his plate and leave all of the ______________________.

DAY 3

I lost my hat. My mother is ______________________ going to be ______________________.

DAY 4

My family and I haven't made definite plans for Saturday afternoon, but we'll ______________________ go to ______________________.

DAY 5

My grandmother doesn't know how to use (the/a/an) ______________________ ______________________ yet. But once she gets used to it, I think she'll ______________________ love it.

TOTAL

clue

SMART START

REVIEW: probably *adverb*

DAY 1

Since my sister doesn't feel well, she'll ______________________

stay home from school and ______________________.

clue *noun*

DAY 2

The mechanic listened to the engine for a ______________________

about what was wrong with the ______________________.

DAY 3

Our teacher gave us a few ______________________ to help us solve

a word problem, so we eventually ______________________

the right answer.

DAY 4

Whenever my mother ______________________, that's always

my first ______________________ that she's feeling annoyed.

DAY 5

In one fairy tale, a wizard gives a prince three ______________________

to solve a puzzle in order to win the ______________________.

TOTAL

REVIEW: clue *noun*

DAY 1

One ____________ that my friend was in a good mood ☐

was seeing her ____________ . ☐

prediction *noun*

DAY 2

Based on our past performance, our coach made a ____________ ☐

that our ____________ team would win Saturday's game. ☐

DAY 3

The cookies smell so good, my ____________ ☐

is that everyone will ____________ them. ☐

DAY 4

My aunt made a ____________ that if it snows ☐

tomorrow, the concert will ____________ . ☐

DAY 5

The teacher asked the students to write their ____________ ☐

about what will happen if it rains during the ____________ . ☐

TOTAL

Toolkit Unit 8 | Argument

Argument

To make an **argument**, explain why you believe something is true by supporting it with convincing reasons, relevant examples, and personal experiences.

 **Find It** **Read the sentences. Underline the best reason, example, or experience to support each argument.**

1. Recycling is good for the environment.
   a. Recycling saves money and energy, and it doesn't add more trash to landfills.
   b. Soda cans can be recycled.
   c. Recycled plastic can be made into other items, such as T-shirts.

2. Young children should get 60 minutes of exercise every day.
   a. I love to play outside because it is fun.
   b. One type of exercise is riding a bike.
   c. In my experience, getting 60 minutes of exercise every day makes me feel stronger and happier.

 **Try It** **Write one convincing reason to support the argument.**

Children shouldn't drink sugary sodas. One important reason is that sugary drinks can cause ______________________.

RATE WORD KNOWLEDGE

Rate how well you know Toolkit words you'll use when you prepare to argue.

RATE IT

BEFORE	3rd Grade	AFTER	4th Grade	5th Grade
1 2 3 4	**discussion**	1 2 3 4	opinion	perspective
1 2 3 4	**believe**	1 2 3 4	fact	persuade
1 2 3 4	**reason**	1 2 3 4	argument	position
1 2 3 4	**agree**	1 2 3 4	convince	reasonable
1 2 3 4	**disagree**	1 2 3 4	evidence	support
1 2 3 4	**experience**	1 2 3 4	convincing	opposing

DISCUSSION GUIDE

- Form groups of four.
- Assign letters to each person. A B D C
- Each group member takes a turn leading a discussion.
- Prepare to report about one word.

DISCUSS WORDS

Discuss how well you know the third grade words. Then, report to the class how you rated each word.

GROUP LEADER Ask

So, _______________ (NAME) what do you know about the word _______________ ?

GROUP MEMBERS Discuss

1 = I **have never seen or heard** the word _______________ . I need to learn what it means.

2 = I **have seen or heard** the word _______________ , but I need to learn the meaning.

3 = I'm **familiar** with the word _______________ . I think it means _______________ .

4 = I **know** the word _______________ . It means _______________ .

REPORTER Report Word Knowledge

Our group gave the word _______________ a rating of _______________ .

SET A GOAL AND REFLECT

First, set a vocabulary goal for this unit by selecting at least two words that you plan to thoroughly learn. At the end of the unit, return to this page and write a reflection about one word you have mastered.

GOAL

During this unit I plan to thoroughly learn the words _______________ and _______________ . Increasing my word knowledge will help me speak and write effectively when I need to argue a point.

REFLECTION

As a result of this unit, I feel most confident about the word _______________ . This is my model sentence: _______________ _______________ .

discussion

noun

Say it: dis • **cus** • sion

 **Write it:** ____________________ **Write it again:** ____________________

____

TOOLKIT

Meaning

a conversation in which people share ideas

Synonym

- conversation

Examples

- The students are having a **discussion** about the chapter that they ____________ .
- During the field trip, the waste ____________ led a **discussion** about recycling.

Forms

- **Singular:** discussion
- **Plural:** discussions

Family

- **Verb:** discuss

Word Partners

- have a discussion about
- a/an (interesting, useful, brief/lengthy) discussion

Examples

- My parents **had a discussion about** inviting my grandmother to move in.
- My brother had **a brief discussion** with the barber about how short to cut his hair.

 **Try It**

- Before riding a new bike, you and your parents should have a **discussion** about how to ride ____________________ .

VERBAL PRACTICE

Talk about it

Discuss
Listen
Write

Discuss ideas with your partner, listen to classmates, and then write your favorite idea.

1. After a long **discussion**, my family decided to visit (a/an) ____________ ____________________ during summer vacation.

2. When I got my report card, my parents and I had a **discussion** about how to improve my ____________________ .

discussion

noun

WRITING PRACTICE

Collaborate
Discuss
Listen
Agree
Write

Discuss ideas with your partner and agree on the best words to complete the frame.

In our class we have had several ____________________ about

____________________________________.

Our Turn
Discuss
Listen
Write

Read the prompt. Work with the teacher to complete the frames. Write a thoughtful response that includes an experience.

PROMPT: Describe a discussion you recently had with a parent, guardian, or relative about something they want you to do.

I recently had a ____________________________________

with my ____________________________________ about

____________________________________.

Be an Academic Author
Write
Discuss
Listen

Read the prompt and complete the frames. Strengthen your response with an example.

PROMPT: What do you and your friends often have discussions about?

My friends and I often have ____________________________________

about ____________________________________,

such as ____________________________________.

Construct a Response
Write
Discuss
Listen

Read the prompt and write a thoughtful response. Strengthen your response with an experience.

PROMPT: Describe a discussion your class recently had about an article or a book. Did you and your classmates enjoy reading it?

____

____

____

grammar tip

Count nouns name things that can be counted. Count nouns have two forms, singular and plural. To make most count nouns plural, add **-s**.

EXAMPLE: The dog's **eyes** are two different **colors**.

believe

verb

Say it: be • lieve

Write it: ______________ ***Write it again:*** ______________

____

TOOLKIT

Meaning

to think that something is true

Synonyms

- to think; to be sure

Examples

- Dentists strongly **believe** that eating __________ is better than eating candy.
- The student **believes** that the field trip to the __________ will be cancelled because of the snow.

Forms

- **Present:**
  I/you/we/they believe
  he/she/it believes
- **Past:** believed

Family

- **Noun:** belief
- **Adjective:** believable, unbelievable

Word Partners

- do not believe that
- strongly believe that

Examples

- Some people **do not believe that** students should wear school uniforms.
- I **strongly believe that** bullying is unacceptable.

Try It

I strongly **believe** that it is important to be ______________ to others.

VERBAL PRACTICE

Talk about it — Discuss / Listen / Write

Discuss ideas with your partner, listen to classmates, and then write your favorite idea.

1. My friend **believes** that all elementary schools should have (a/an) ______________

______________.

2. Crossing guards strongly **believe** that elementary students should

______________ before crossing the street.

believe

verb

WRITING PRACTICE

Collaborate
Discuss
Listen
Agree
Write

Discuss ideas with your partner and agree on the best words to complete the frame.

We strongly ______________ that little children should learn ______________________ before they start kindergarten.

Our Turn
Discuss
Listen
Write

Read the prompt. Work with the teacher to complete the frames. Write a thoughtful response that includes a reason.

PROMPT: Do you believe that every child should own a pet?

I (do/do not) __________ ______________ that every child should own a pet. One important reason is that some children (are/are not) ______________ ______________________________.

Be an Academic Author
Write
Discuss
Listen

Read the prompt and complete the frames. Strengthen your response with a reason.

PROMPT: Do you believe that third graders should be able to stay up late on school nights?

I (do/do not) __________ ______________ that third graders should be able to stay up late on school nights. One reason is that third graders need time to ______________________________.

Construct a Response
Write
Discuss
Listen

Read the prompt and write a thoughtful response. Strengthen your response with a reason.

PROMPT: Some students believe that students should have a day off from school on their birthday. What do you believe?

____

____

____

grammar tip

The **helping verb *should*** tells about something you believe needs to happen. When you use the word ***should***, add a verb in the base form.

EXAMPLE: I believe that children **should** exercise every day.

reason

noun

Say it: rea • son

 ***Write it:*** ______________ ***Write it again:*** ______________

 ______________

TOOLKIT

Meaning
a fact that explains why you do something, or why something happens

Synonym
- explanation

Examples
- The **reason** we have to be quiet is that the ______________ is sleeping.

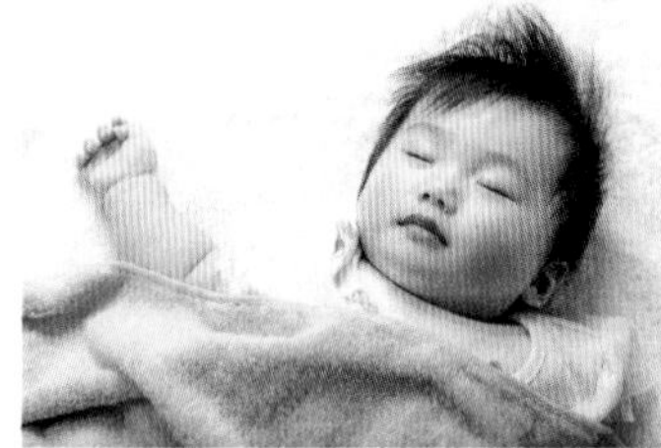

- Some siblings argue over the ______________ remote for silly **reasons**.

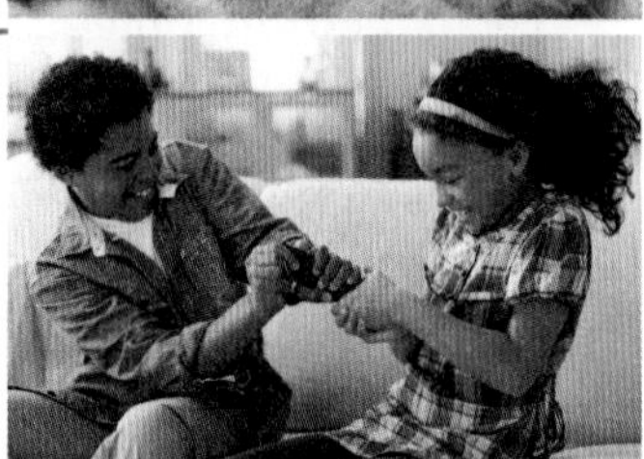

Forms
- **Singular:** reason
- **Plural:** reasons

Family

Word Partners
- give a reason for something
- a good/convincing reason

Examples
- My teacher asked me to **give a reason for** not finishing my worksheet.
- One **good reason** to stay up late on the 4th of July is to see the fireworks.

 **Try It**

One good **reason** for feeling grumpy is not getting enough ______________ .

VERBAL PRACTICE

Talk about it — Discuss / Listen / Write

Discuss ideas with your partner, listen to classmates, and then write your favorite idea.

1. The **reason** school was closed last month was because of the ______________ .

2. My mother had a good **reason** for pouring the milk down the drain. It was ______________ .

reason

noun

WRITING PRACTICE

Collaborate
Discuss
Listen
Agree
Write

Discuss ideas with your partner and agree on the best words to complete the frame.

A convincing ______________________ for being late to school is ______________________.

Our Turn
Discuss
Listen
Write

Read the prompt. Work with the teacher to complete the frames. Write a thoughtful response that includes a reason.

PROMPT: Think about your favorite movie. What is one good reason why it is your favorite?

My favorite movie is ______________________.

The ______________________ it is my favorite movie is that it is ______________________.

Be an Academic Author
Write
Discuss
Listen

Read the prompt and complete the frames. Strengthen your response with an experience.

PROMPT: Describe a time you had to cancel a plan or miss a party. Did you have a good reason?

Once I was supposed to ______________________, but I wasn't able to do it. I had a good ______________________. I couldn't do it because I was too ______________________.

Construct a Response
Read
Discuss
Listen

Read the prompt and write a thoughtful response. Strengthen your response with a reason.

PROMPT: Think about something you aren't allowed to do. What is the reason?

____

____

____

grammar tip

A **common noun** names a person, place, thing, or idea. **Singular nouns** name one person, place, thing, or idea. The words *a*, *an*, and *the* often appear before a singular noun.

EXAMPLE: I had an **idea** for a **song** to sing for the **show**.

agree

verb

Say it: a • gree

 ***Write it:*** ______________ ***Write it again:*** ______________

 ______________

TOOLKIT

Meaning

to think that something is right, or to think the same way as someone else

Antonym

- disagree

Examples

- Many children **agree** that playing in a ______________ is a lot of fun.

- At the animal shelter, the whole family **agreed** on which ______________ to take home.

Forms

- **Present**
  I/You/We/They agree
  He/She/It agrees
- **Past** agreed

Family

- **Noun:** agreement

Word Partners

- agree on something
- agree totally/completely

Examples

- Yesterday, my parents **agreed on what to make for dinner**.
- My friends think soccer is exciting, and I **agree totally**.

 **Try It**

My brother thinks ______________ is the best ice cream flavor, and I **agree** completely.

VERBAL PRACTICE

Talk about it Discuss ideas with your partner, listen to classmates, and then write your favorite idea.

Discuss
Listen
Write

1. My friends and I **agree** that our cafeteria makes good ______________.

2. When my friend and I don't **agree** on something, we try not to get ______________ with each other.

WRITING PRACTICE

Collaborate
Discuss
Listen
Agree
Write

Discuss ideas with your partner and agree on the best words to complete the frame.

We all ______________________________ completely that gym class is

______________________________.

Our Turn
Discuss
Listen
Write

Read the prompt. Work with the teacher to complete the frames. Write a response that includes an experience.

PROMPT: Think about a book that you read and enjoyed, but your friend did not enjoy. Explain why you do not agree with your friend's reaction to the book.

My friend and I both read ______________________, but (he/she) __________

did not enjoy it. However, I do not ____________________ because I thought the

book was ______________________________, especially the character

______________________________.

Be an Academic Author
Write
Discuss
Listen

Read the prompt and complete the frames. Strengthen your response with a reason.

PROMPT: Some people think watching television is bad for kids. Do you agree totally?

I (do/do not) ____________________ ____________________ totally

with the idea that watching television is bad for kids. The reason I think this is

because many programs can be ______________________________.

Construct a Response
Read
Discuss
Listen

Read the prompt and write a thoughtful response. Strengthen your response with an experience.

PROMPT: Think of a time you and a classmate had to agree on a writing assignment. What did you agree on?

____

____

____

grammar tip

An **adverb** describes an action. Adverbs usually end in ***-ly*** and come after the verb to describe how the action is done.

EXAMPLE: I did **poorly** on the last test, so I'm going to study **carefully** before the next one.

disagree

verb

Say it: dis • a • **gree**

 ***Write it:*** ______________ ***Write it again:*** ______________

 ______________

Meaning

to think differently about something than someone else

Antonym

- agree

Examples

- My brother thinks hamburgers are __________, but my sister strongly **disagrees**.

- Many people think __________ days are awful, but my friend **disagrees**.

TOOLKIT

Forms

- **Present**
  I/You/We/They disagree
  He/She/It disagrees
- **Past** disagreed

Family

- **Noun:** disagreement

Word Partners

- disagree with ____ about ____
- strongly disagree

Examples

- My uncle thinks electronics are bad, but I **disagree with him about video games**.
- Some people think smoking is OK, but I **strongly disagree**.

 **Try It**

My aunt thinks pets are messy, but I **disagree** because our ______________ is very clean.

VERBAL PRACTICE

Talk about it **Discuss ideas with your partner, listen to classmates, and then write your favorite idea.**

Discuss
Listen
Write

1. I often **disagree** with my friend about ______________.

2. Even if I strongly **disagree** with someone, I never say that their ideas are ______________.

WRITING PRACTICE

Collaborate

Discuss
Listen
Agree
Write

Discuss ideas with your partner and agree on the best words to complete the frame.

When you strongly ______________________ with someone about going to the ______________________ without an adult, it is important to say something.

Our Turn

Discuss
Listen
Write

Read the prompt. Work with the teacher to complete the frames. Write a thoughtful response that includes a reason.

PROMPT: Think of someone who likes one subject in school that isn't your favorite. Explain why you disagree.

My ______________________ thinks ______________________ is the best subject in school, but I ______________________. I think ______________________ is the best because you can learn about ______________________ during this subject.

Be an Academic Author

Write
Discuss
Listen

Read the prompt and complete the frames. Strengthen your response with a reason.

PROMPT: Think of a singer that you and a friend have different views about. Why do you disagree with your friend?

My friend thinks ______________________ is a ______________________ singer. I strongly ______________________ because I think this singer is really ______________________.

Construct a Response

Read
Discuss
Listen

Read the prompt and write a thoughtful response. Strengthen your response with a reason.

PROMPT: What is something that you and your parents disagree about?

____

____

____

grammar tip

Count nouns name things that can be counted. Count nouns have two forms, singular and plural. To make most count nouns plural, add **-s**.

EXAMPLE: I like to express **ideas** and **opinions** with my friends.

experience

noun

Say it: ex • **pe** • ri • ence

 ***Write it:*** ______________________ ***Write it again:*** ______________________

 ______________________

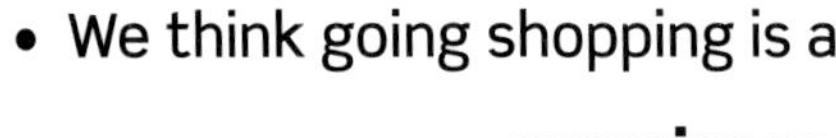

TOOLKIT

Meaning
something that happens to you or something that you do, that has an effect on what you think or do

Synonym
- event

Examples
- My uncle used to be a chef so he has a lot of **experience** with ____________ .

- We think going shopping is a ____________ **experience**.

Forms
- **Singular:** experience
- **Plural:** experiences

Family
- **Verb:** experience

Word Partners
- have experience with ___
- recent/personal experience

Examples
- I **have experience with** computers.
- My sister had a **personal experience** with a newborn kitten.

 **Try It**

I have **experience** with ______________________________________ a dog.

VERBAL PRACTICE

Talk about it **Discuss ideas with your partner, listen to classmates, and then write your favorite idea.**

Discuss
Listen
Write

1. I had a recent **experience** ______________________________________

______________________ at the beach.

2. I have some **experience** in the kitchen, which is why I can make (a/an) __________

______________________________________ .

experience

noun

WRITING PRACTICE

Collaborate

Discuss
Listen
Agree
Write

Discuss ideas with your partner and agree on the best words to complete the frame.

Many third graders have ______________ playing team sports like ______________.

Our Turn

Discuss
Listen
Write

Read the prompt. Work with the teacher to complete the frames. Write a thoughtful response that includes an experience.

PROMPT: Tell about a recent positive experience you had at school.

Recently, I had a positive ______________ at school. This happened when I ______________.

Be an Academic Author

Write
Discuss
Listen

Read the prompt and complete the frames. Strengthen your response with an example.

PROMPT: What is something that you have had several experiences doing?

I have had several ______________ working with ______________. For example, I often ______________.

Construct a Response

Read
Discuss
Listen

Read the prompt and write a thoughtful response. Strengthen your response with an experience.

PROMPT: Describe something fun that you recently experienced with some friends or family members.

____

____

____

grammar tip

Quantity adjectives tell "how much" or "how many." Quantity adjectives go before a plural noun. Common quantity adjectives are: *most, many, some, several,* and *both.*

EXAMPLE: Most students bring lunch from home, but **many** buy lunch in the cafeteria.

discussion

SMART START

REVIEW: prediction *noun*

DAY 1

Before the summer, my mother made a ________________ that I'd learn how to ________________ by the end of the summer, and I did!

discussion *noun*

DAY 2

My friend and I had a ________________ about the ________________ after we finished watching it.

DAY 3

After my dentist found cavities, my parents and I had a ________________ about me needing to eat less ________________.

DAY 4

During our many class ________________, I sometimes feel ________________ about offering my ideas in front of a large group.

DAY 5

When I received $50 for my birthday, my best friend and I had a ________________ about whether I should save the money or spent it on ________________.

TOTAL

REVIEW: discussion *noun*

DAY 1

We had a class ______________ today about

the ______________ we just read.

believe *verb*

DAY 2

My grandmother strongly ______________ that it is wrong to

waste ______________ .

DAY 3

I ______________ that the TV show

____

is educational because it teaches young children about school subjects.

DAY 4

I ______________ that everyone should

______________ to help keep the Earth healthy.

DAY 5

Our teacher ______________ that it is important for us to

______________ in school.

TOTAL

reason

REVIEW: believe *verb*

DAY 1

I ______________________ that animals have feelings. For example, when dogs wag their tails, I think they are showing that they feel ______________________.

reason *noun*

DAY 2

My friends were arguing for a silly ______________________. They both wanted the bigger piece of ______________________.

DAY 3

I have a good ______________________ for not being hungry. It's because I just ______________________.

DAY 4

The ______________________ I don't like to lend people my favorite book is that I don't want it to get ______________________.

DAY 5

The ______________________ the toy is broken is that the toddler ______________________ it.

TOTAL

REVIEW: reason *noun*

DAY 1

One of the many ______________________ I like to go to my aunt's house is that she has a ______________________ in her backyard.

agree *verb*

DAY 2

My friend thinks that the computer game ______________________ ______________________ is great, and I ______________________ completely.

DAY 3

When my friend and I don't ______________________ on something, we take time to ______________________ each other's views.

DAY 4

Last week, my father and I ______________________ on a list of chores for me to do, including ______________________.

DAY 5

My friend thinks wearing ______________________ is cool and I ______________________ totally.

TOTAL

disagree

REVIEW: agree *verb*

DAY 1

My sister thinks movies about cartoon princesses are ______________________,

and I totally ______________________.

disagree *verb*

DAY 2

You can strongly ______________________ with someone about

something but still really ______________________ that person.

DAY 3

My brother and I always ______________________ on what to order

for dinner when my family gets takeout. I usually want pizza, but he usually

wants ______________________.

DAY 4

I think roller coasters are fun, but my cousin ______________________

with me. He thinks they're ______________________.

DAY 5

Some children my age think that the ______________________

museum is boring, but I ______________________.

I think it's fascinating.

TOTAL

REVIEW: disagree *verb*

DAY 1

My friend thinks that ______________________ tastes terrible, but I ______________________________________.

experience *noun*

DAY 2

Riding (a/an) ________ ______________________ can be a scary but amazing ______________________________________.

DAY 3

My cousin has a lot of ______________________ with dancing, as she has taken ballet and ____________________ classes since she was five years old.

DAY 4

Our class has ______________________ doing different kinds of math problems, such as addition and ______________________.

DAY 5

I would like to ______________________ someday because I think it would be an exciting ______________________________.

TOTAL

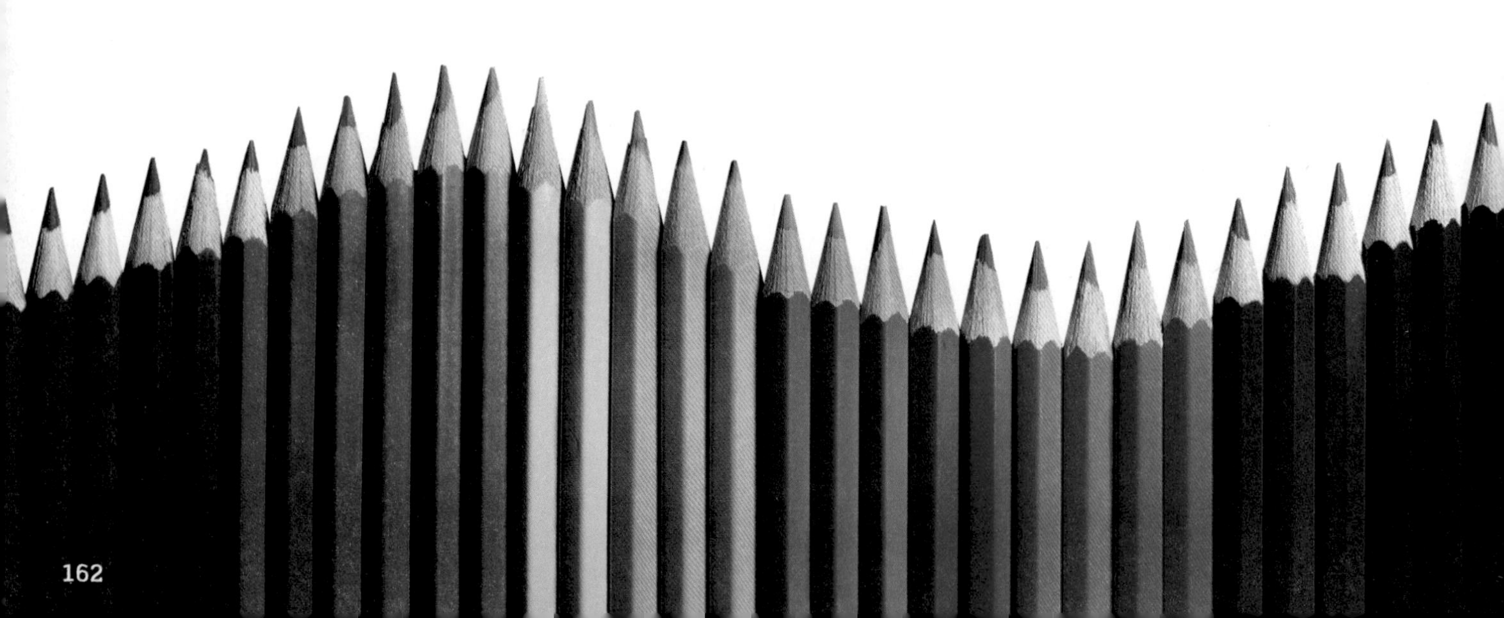

grammar lessons

grammar

Present Tense Verbs

Use the **present tense** when you talk about actions that happen usually, sometimes, or regularly.

	Subject	Verb
Use the **base form** of the verb when the subject is *I, you, we,* or *they.*	I You We They	**run** quickly base form
Use the **-s** form of the verb when the subject is *he, she,* or *it.*	He She It	**runs** quickly -s form

- When the base form of the verb ends in **s, sh, ch, x,** or **o,** add ***-es:***
  miss → ***misses***; ***wash*** → ***washes***; ***catch*** → ***catches***; ***fix*** → ***fixes***; ***go*** → ***goes***
- When the base form of the verb ends in a consonant + ***y***, change the ***y*** to ***i*** and add ***-es: cry*** → ***cries***

Find It

Read the sentences. Write the correct form of the present tense verb.

1. I (speak/speaks) ______________________ Spanish with my grandmother.
2. The President (live/lives) ______________________ in the White House.
3. Her cousin (come/comes) ______________________ for a visit every summer.
4. The earth (go/goes) ______________________ around the sun once a year.

Try It

Complete the sentences using the correct form of the verb.

1. My teacher (give) ______________________ homework on Wednesdays.
2. The tree's leaves (turn) ______________________ red in the fall.
3. My best friend and I (meet) ______________________ in the cafeteria every day.
4. My mother (take) ______________________ me clothes shopping in September.

Discuss and Write

Collaborate Discuss Agree Write Listen

Work with a partner. Use the correct form of the verbs to complete the sentences.

1. wake up/ sleep — I ________________ early on school days, but ________________ late on the weekend.

2. wear/ smell — My mother ________________ a perfume that ________________ like roses.

3. eat/leave — The child ________________ all her rice first and ________________ her vegetables for last.

4. listen/ study — My brother ________________ to music while he ________________.

Your Turn Think Write

Work independently. Use the correct form of the verbs and your own words to complete the sentences.

1. eat — On Thanksgiving, people ________________ special food like ________________.

2. add — When my father makes salad, he ________________ a lot of ________________.

3. sleeps — My cat ________________ (in/on) ________________ my ________________.

4. like — I ________________ stories about ________________.

grammar

Past Tense Verbs

Use the **past tense** to talk about events or actions that have already happened.

Subject	Base Form of Verb + *-ed/-d*	
I He She It You We They	play**ed**	all day yesterday.

- To form the simple past tense of most regular verbs, add ***-ed*** to the base form of the verb: ***listen*** → ***listened***
- For regular verbs that end in *-e*, add ***-d***: ***smile*** → ***smiled***

Find It

Read the sentences. Complete the sentences using the correct form of the verb.

1. Last year, Tom (start/started) ____________________ a band with a friend.
2. We often (order/ordered) ____________________ books online.
3. Every summer, we (visit/visited) ____________________ family in Mexico.
4. Our teacher (smile/smiled) ____________________ when she opened the card we made for her.

Try It

Complete the sentences using the past tense form of the verb.

1. My mother (bake) ____________________ a triple chocolate cake for my birthday.
2. We (return) ____________________ the shirt because it didn't fit well.
3. Our neighbor (adopt) ____________________ the cutest kitten last week!

Discuss and Write

Collaborate **Work with a partner. Use the correct form of the verbs to complete the sentences.**

Discuss
Agree
Write
Listen

1. receive/miss — After I ____________________ my grandfather's e-mail yesterday, I ____________________ him even more.

2. borrow/renew — A couple of months ago I ____________________ a book from the library and, because I liked it so much, I ____________________ it three times.

3. watch/hatch — Yesterday on a field trip to a farm, my class ____________________ a baby bird as it ____________________ from its egg.

Your Turn **Work independently. Use the correct form of the verbs and your own words to complete the sentences.**

Think
Write

1. sprain — I ____________________ my ankle while I was playing ____.

2. cry — My baby sister ____________________ when my mother wouldn't let her have (a/an) ____________________ ____.

3. plant — My father and I ____________________ ____________________ in our garden last Saturday.

grammar

Present Progressive Tense

Use the **present progressive tense** to talk about an action that is happening right now.

Subject	*be*	Verb + *ing*
I	am	eat**ing** dinner.
He She It	is	
You We They	are	

- To form the progressive tense of most verbs, add ***-ing*** to the base form of the verb: read → ***reading***
- For verbs that end in a consonant + ***-e***, drop the ***-e*** before adding ***-ing:*** dance → ***dancing***

Find It

Complete the sentences using the correct form of the verb.

1. I am (play) ______________________ tag with my friends right now.

2. The librarian is (help) ______________________ me look for a book.

3. The birds are (make) ______________________ a nest in the tree.

Try It

Read the present tense sentences. Write the sentences as present progressive sentences.

1. The teacher asks questions.

____

2. We buy ice cream cones.

____

3. The lunch line moves very slowly.

____

Discuss and Write

Collaborate **Work with a partner. Use the correct form of the verbs to complete the sentences.**

Discuss
Agree
Write
Listen

1. sing/jump The kindergarteners are __________________ a song and __________________ around.

2. click/open I'm __________________ on the link on the web page, but it isn't __________________.

3. hide/try My friend is __________________ and I'm __________________ to find him.

Your Turn **Work independently. Use the correct form of the verbs and your own words to complete the sentences.**

Think
Write

1. The mechanic is (fix) __________________ the engine of the __________________.

2. I'm (pack) __________________ a __________________ for the sleepover at my friend's house tonight.

3. It's (rain) __________________ outside, so you should take (a/an) __________________ __________________.

4. She is (close) __________________ the window because it is too __________________ outside.

grammar

Adjectives

An adjective describes a noun and gives more information about it. It usually comes before the noun it describes.

Adjective	Example
large	America is a **large** country.
soft	My hamster has **soft** fur.
fun	It was a **fun** game.

An adjective can also come directly after verbs such as *is, am, are, was, were, looks, tastes, feels.*
The boat is **large.** / The movie was **funny.** / The fruit looks **fresh.** / The salsa tastes **spicy.**

Find It

Find and underline the adjective in each sentence.

1. The child couldn't reach the high shelf.
2. My aunt made a chocolate cake for my birthday.
3. I can't take a shower because we ran out of hot water!
4. When she and her family visited Los Angeles, they saw some famous people.

Try It

Rewrite each sentence, placing the adjective in the correct place.

1. (blue) I need the marker.

____

2. (spicy) I don't like to eat pizza.

____

3. (warm) We wear jackets in the winter.

____

Discuss and Write

Collaborate (Discuss, Agree, Write, Listen) **Work with a partner. Complete the sentences by putting each adjective in the correct place.**

1. (big, cold) May I please have a ________________ glass of ________________ lemonade?

2. (beautiful, favorite) My ________________ singer has a ________________ voice.

3. (delicious, ripe) The most ________________ food is ________________ mangoes.

4. (sweet, yellow) The ________________ flowers have a ________________ smell.

Your Turn (Think, Write) **Work independently. Add your own adjective to complete each sentence.**

1. My best friend is a very ________________ person.

2. There was ________________ music coming from the house next door.

3. Our teacher downloaded two ________________ apps on our computers yesterday.

4. When I grow up, I'd like to have (a/an) ________________ ________________ car.

grammar

Adverbs

An adverb describes a verb and gives more information about it.

Adverb	Example
clearly	Our teacher speaks **clearly.**
correctly	I answered the question **correctly.**
slowly	Please spell the word **slowly.**

An adverb usually comes after the verb it describes. Most adverbs are formed by adding *-ly* to an adjective: ***clear* → *clearly; correct* → *correctly; slow* → *slowly***

Find It

Find and underline the adverb in each sentence.

1. You must speak quietly when you're in a library.

2. The baby crawled across the floor slowly.

3. Our cat purrs loudly when we pet him behind his ears.

4. My dentist said I should brush and floss my teeth carefully each day.

Try It

Read the first sentence. Look at the underlined adjective. Then complete the second sentence, using the adverb form of the adjective.

1. The line is slow. The line is moving ______________________.

2. We were truthful. We answered the question ______________________.

3. Their singing is loud. They sing ______________________.

4. He is a professional baseball player. He plays baseball ______________________.

Discuss and Write

Collaborate **Work with a partner. Complete the sentences with either the adjective or the adverb.**

Discuss
Agree
Write
Listen

1. (close/closely) While my dance teacher did the steps, I watched ________________________.

2. (beautiful/beautifully) That is a ____________________ bunch of flowers.

3. (sad/sadly) My friend told me the ____________________ news.

4. (quick/quickly) Don't eat too ____________________ or you'll get a stomachache.

Your Turn **Work independently. Add your own adverb to complete each sentence.**

Think
Write

1. I knocked on the door ____________________ until someone answered.
2. She drove ____________________ during her driving test.
3. We always speak to our teachers ____________________.
4. I held my new baby brother ____________________.

grammar

Adverbs of Frequency

Use **adverbs of frequency** to talk about how often actions happen.

	Adverbs of Frequency	Examples with the Verb *Be*	Examples with Other Verbs
100%	always	I **am always** polite.	I **always speak** politely.
↕	usually	She **is usually** early.	She **usually comes** to school early.
	sometimes	They **are sometimes** tired.	They **sometimes look** tired.
0%	never	My little brother **is never** quiet.	My little brother **never talks** quietly.

- Put adverbs of frequency after the verb ***be***.
- Put adverbs of frequency before all other verbs.

Find It

Find and underline the adverb of frequency in each sentence.

1. I never drink soda because it's not healthy.
2. Our bus driver always says hello when we get on the bus.
3. My parents sometimes let me stay up late on the weekend.
4. Jane usually wears her hair in a ponytail, but today she's wearing it down for picture day.

Try It

Read the pairs of sentences. Underline the sentence that has the adverb of frequency in the correct place.

1. We sometimes go to the park after school. | We go sometimes to the park after school.
2. The baby is usually tired in the afternoon. | The baby usually is tired in the afternoon.
3. She wears dresses never. | She never wears dresses.
4. My school always has a field day in the spring. | My school has a field day always in the spring.

Discuss and Write

Collaborate **Work with a partner. Complete the sentences using appropriate adverbs of frequency.**

Discuss
Agree
Write
Listen

1. My parents drink coffee in the morning, but I ________________ do!

2. We ________________ have a spelling test on Friday, but this week we didn't.

3. My friend ________________ buys lunch in the cafeteria, but more often she brings lunch from home.

4. Our teacher put our names on our seat, so we ________________ sit in the same chairs every day.

Your Turn **Work independently. Complete the sentences using appropriate adverbs of frequency and your own words.**

Think
Write

1. We ________________ watch ________________ because it's our favorite TV show.

2. My cousin and I sometimes argue, but we're ________________ ________________ friends.

3. I ________________ eat ________________ because I really don't like it.

4. My parents ________________ bake ________________, but most of the time they just buy (it/them) ________________ at the supermarket.

grammar

Possessive Nouns

Use possessive nouns to show that something belongs to someone or something.

	Singular Noun	Possessive Noun	Example
To show that something belongs to someone or something, add an apostrophe (') and **-s** to a singular noun.	girl	girl**'s**	The girl**'s** backpack is empty.
	Plural Noun that ends in -s	**Possessive Noun**	**Example**
To show that something belongs to more than one person or thing, add an apostrophe (') at the end of a plural noun, following the -s.	boys	boys**'**	The boys**'** uniforms are green.

Find It

Complete the sentences using the correct possessive noun.

1. I really like my art (teacher's/teachers') ______________________ handwriting.
2. The judges looked at all of the (student's/students') ______________________ artwork before deciding on the winner of the competition.
3. My two (sister's/sisters') ______________________ voices sound a lot alike.
4. The (dog's/dogs') ______________________ eyes are two different colors. One is blue and the other is brown.

Try It

Complete the sentences with the correct possessive form of the noun.

1. All of my (friends) ______________________ families are really nice.
2. (Sonia) ______________________ teacher gives a lot of homework.
3. Last summer I visited a stable and got to brush all of the (horses) ______________________ manes.

Discuss and Write

Collaborate
Discuss
Agree
Write
Listen

Work with a partner. Read the first sentence. Then complete the second sentence with the correct possessive noun.

1. The scent of the flowers is beautiful.

   The ____________________ scent is beautiful.

2. The wheels of the toy truck fell off.

   The toy ____________________ wheels fell off.

3. The collar of the dog is too tight.

   The ____________________ collar is too tight.

4. The uniforms of the boys got dirty during the game.

   The ____________________ uniforms got dirty during the game.

Your Turn
Think
Write

Work independently. Complete the sentences with the correct possessive form of the noun and your own words.

1. (friend) My best ____________________ little sister loves to ____.

2. (cousin) There was cake and ____________________ at my ____________________ party.

3. (neighbors) Both of my ____________________ houses have ____________________ windows.

4. (toddlers) All of the ____________________ ____________________ were scattered on the floor until the teacher asked the toddlers to pick them up.

grammar

There, Their, They're

There, their, and **they're** are homophones. Homophones are words that have the same sound but are spelled differently and have different meanings.

Word	Explanation	Example
there	*There* is an adverb that means *that place.* *There* is also used with the verbs *is, are, was,* and *were* at the beginning of a sentence or clause.	The toy store is over **there.** **There** are 50 states in America.
their	*Their* shows ownership. It is always followed by a noun.	Our neighbors painted **their** house.
they're	*They're* is the short form of the words *they + are.*	**They're** riding bicycles together.

Find It

Choose the correct word to complete the sentences.

1. Can you help me move the boxes? (Their/They're) ______________________ heavy.
2. They were late to school because they missed (their/there) ______________________ bus.
3. (Their/There) ______________________ are 26 letters in the English alphabet.
4. My aunt and her boyfriend are going to get married. I'm going to be a bridesmaid at (there/their) ______________________ wedding.

Try It

Complete the sentences using *there, their,* or *they're.*

1. John and Orla have been taking karate classes for years. ______________________ earning blue belts this year!
2. The children ate hot fudge sundaes, and now ______________________ faces are covered in ice cream.
3. Somebody spilled milk over ______________________ .

Discuss and Write

Collaborate **Work with a partner. Complete the sentences using *there, their,* and *they're.***

Discuss
Agree
Write
Listen

1. They got ______________ dog from an animal shelter. He was the friendliest dog ______________.

2. ______________ trying to get tickets to the baseball game because ______________ favorite team is playing.

3. Look at the hive! Hundreds of bees store ______________ honey in ______________.

Your Turn **Work independently. Complete the sentences with *there, their,* and *they're* and your own words.**

Think
Write

1. These shoes are too ______________.
______________ uncomfortable.

2. ______________ mother works as a ______________.

3. Amalia and Ayesha made a ______________ together. Look! It's over ______________.

4. The two TV programs I like most are ______________ and ______________. ______________ the best, in my opinion.

Acknowledgments, continued from page ii

vi (t) ©Andy Z/Shutterstock.com, (cr) ©Ariel Skelley/Getty Images, (cl) ©Hero Images/Digital Vision/Getty Images, (b) ©bikeriderlondon/ Shutterstock.com. **viii** (t) ©paulaphoto/ Shutterstock.com, (cr) ©Kamira/Shutterstock. com, (cl) ©holbox/Shutterstock.com, (b) ©WARNER BROS. PICTURES/ALSBIRK BLID/ Album/Newscom. **x** (t) ©Steve Goodwin/Getty Images, (cr) ©KidStock/Blend Images/Getty Images, (cl) ©AVAVA/Shutterstock.com, (b) ©Jose Luis Pelaez Inc/Blend Images/ Getty Images. **2** ©Jacek Chabraszewski/ Shutterstock.com. **4** (t) ©Schubbel/ Shutterstock.com, (b) ©Markus Mainka/ Shutterstock.com. **6** (t) ©saisnaps/Shutterstock. com, (b) ©Nikolai Pozdeev/Shutterstock.com. **8** (t) ©spotmatik/Shutterstock.com, (b) ©Anup Shah/Digital Vision/Getty Images. **10** (t) ©Rob Marmion/Shutterstock.com, (b) ©Pressmaster/Shutterstock.com. **12** (t) ©Michael Pettigrew/Shutterstock.com, (b) ©Monkey Business Images/Shutterstock. com. **14** (t) ©gorillaimages/Shutterstock.com, (b) ©Vadym Zaitsev/Shutterstock.com. **22** (l) ©rachisan alexandra/Shutterstock.com, (r) ©M Swiet Productions/Getty Images. **24** (t) ©Monkey Business Images/Shutterstock. com, (b) ©Ionescu Alexandru/Shutterstock.com. **26** (t) ©Nastya Glazneva/Shutterstock.com, (b) ©Olesya Feketa/Shutterstock.com. **28** (t) ©muratart/Shutterstock.com, (b) ©muratart/ Shutterstock.com. **30** (t) ©Andresr/ Shutterstock.com, (b) ©Alinute Silzeviciute/ Shutterstock.com. **32** (t) ©Geoff Hardy/ Shutterstock.com, (b) ©photobar/Shutterstock. com. **34** (t) ©stoykovic/Shutterstock.com, (b) ©Jaimie Duplass/Shutterstock.com. **42** ©wavebreakmedia/Shutterstock.com. **44** (t) ©wavebreakmedia/Shutterstock.com, (b) ©Michelle D. Milliman/Shutterstock.com. **46** (t) ©Monkey Business Images/Shutterstock. com, (b) ©Johnny Greig/E+/Getty Images. **48** (t) ©Ariel Skelley/Getty Images, (b) ©Patricia Chumillas/Shutterstock.com. **50** (t) ©Fer Gregory/Shutterstock.com, (b) ©Eric Isselee/ Shutterstock.com. **52** (t) ©Zurijeta/Shutterstock. com, (b) ©fontina/Moment Open/Getty Images. **54** (t) ©Poznyakov/Shutterstock.com, (b) ©Andy Z/Shutterstock.com. **62** ©jps/Shutterstock.com. **64** (t) ©Janine Wiedel Photolibrary/Alamy, (b) ©Pressmaster/Shutterstock.com. **66** (t) ©michaeljung/Shutterstock.com, (b) ©Yellow Dog Productions/Getty Images. **68** (t) ©3445128471/Shutterstock.com, (b) ©Craig Hanson/Shutterstock.com. **70** (t) ©Hero Images/Digital Vision/Getty Images, (b) Fotokostic/Shutterstock.com. **72** (t) ©Westend61/Getty Images, (b) ©Andresr/ Shutterstock.com. **74** (t) ©Alexey Losevich/ Shutterstock.com, (b) ©bikeriderlondon/ Shutterstock.com. **82** ©Kamira/Shutterstock. com. **84** (t) ©Karen Struthers/Shutterstock.com, (b) ©fatihhoca/Getty Images. **86** (t) ©George Doyle/Getty Images, (b) ©KPG Payless2/ Shutterstock.com. **88** (t) ©Jonathan Knowles/ Getty Images, (b) ©paulaphoto/Shutterstock. com. **90** (t) ©Ljupco Smokovski/Shutterstock. com, (b) ©Blend Images/Alamy. **92** (b) ©Diego Cervo/Shutterstock.com, (b) ©Steve Cukrov/Shutterstock.com. **94** (t) ©Tom Wang/Shutterstock.com, (b) ©Andy Dean Photography/Shutterstock.com. **102** ©Martin Dworschak/Shutterstock.com. **104** (t) ©Tui De Roy/Getty Images, (bl) ©Paul Stringer/Shutterstock.com, (br) ©megastocker/ Shutterstock.com. **106** (t) ©Gertan/ Shutterstock.com, (b) ©Eric Isselee/Shutterstock. com. **108** (tl) ©tratong/Shutterstock.com, (tr) ©Dave Pusey/Shutterstock.com, (bl) ©fstockfoto/Shutterstock.com, (br) ©Vacclav/ Shutterstock.com. **110** (t) ©holbox/ Shutterstock.com, (bl) ©vblinov/Shutterstock. com, (br) ©Nicole Aletta Planken-Kooij/ iStockphoto. **112** (t) ©Goodluz/Shutterstock. com, (b) ©WARNER BROS. PICTURES/ALSBIRK BLID/Album/Newscom. **114** (t) ©Nailia Schwarz/Shutterstock.com, (b) ©James Woodson/Digital Vision/Getty Images. **122** ©Algefoto/Shutterstock.com. **124** (t) ©Frannyanne/Shutterstock.com, (b) ©Jose Gil/Shutterstock.com. **126** (t) ©Malte Pott/ Shutterstock.com, (b) ©Richard Peterson / Shutterstock.com. **128** (t) ©KidStock/Blend Images/Getty Images, (b) ©PhotoAlto/ Eric Audras/Getty Images. **130** (t) ©Image Source/Getty Images, (b) ©Xpacifica/National Geographic Creative. **132** (t) ©Tommy Olofsson/ Alamy Limited, (b) ©Syda Productions/ Shutterstock.com. **134** (t) ©RTimages/ Shutterstock.com, (b) ©Steve Goodwin/Getty Images. **142** ©AVAVA/Shutterstock.com. **144** (t) ©Jose Luis Pelaez Inc/Blend Images/ Getty Images, (b) ©Arthur Tilley/Getty Images. **146** (t) ©Connie Lanyon-Roberts/Shutterstock. com, (b) ©Zurijeta/Shutterstock.com. **148** (t) ©leungchopan/Shutterstock.com, (b) ©KidStock/Blend Images/Getty Images. **150** (t) ©Golden Pixels LLC/Shutterstock.com, (b) ©Susan Schmitz/Shutterstock.com. **152** (t) ©Fabiana Ponzi/Shutterstock.com, (b) ©Patrick Foto/Shutterstock.com. **154** (t) © Hasloo Group Production Studio/ Shutterstock.com, (b) ©Image Source/Getty Images.